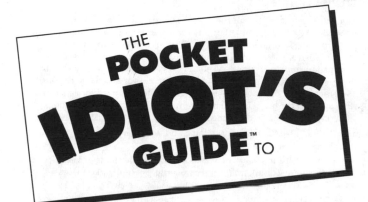

THE
POCKET
IDIOT'S
GUIDE™ TO

French

by Gail Stein

alpha
books

A Division of Macmillan General Reference
A Pearson Education Macmillan Company
1633 Broadway, New York, NY 10019-6785

THE POCKET IDIOT'S GUIDE TO name and design are registered trademarks of Macmillan, Inc.

Macmillan Publishing books may be purchased for business or sales promotional use. For information please write: Special Markets Department, Macmillan Publishing USA, 1633 Broadway, New York, NY 10019.

International Standard Book Number: 0-02-863146-3
Library of Congress Catalog Card Number: available upon request

01 00   8 7 6 5 4 3 2

Interpretation of the printing code: the rightmost number of the first series of numbers is the year of the book's printing; the rightmost number of the second series of numbers is the number of the book's printing. For example, a printing code of 99-1 shows that the first printing occurred in 1999.

Printed in the United States of America

Note: This publication contains the opinions and ideas of its author. It is intended to provide helpful and informative material on the subject matter covered. It is sold with the understanding that the author and publisher are not engaged in rendering professional services in the book. If the reader requires personal assistance or advice, a competent professional should be consulted.

The author and publisher specifically disclaim any responsibility for any liability, loss or risk, personal or otherwise, which is incurred as a consequence, directly or indirectly, of the use and application of any of the contents of this book.

Publisher: Kathy Nebenhaus
Editorial Director: Gary M. Krebs
Managing Editor: Bob Shuman
Marketing Brand Manager: Felice Primeau
Acquisitions Editor: Jessica Faust
Development Editors: Phil Kitchel, Amy Zavatto
Assistant Editor: Georgette Blau
Production Editor: Jenaffer Brandt
Cover Designer: Mike Freeland
Photo Editor: Richard H. Fox
Illustrator: Floyd Hughes
Book Designer: Nathan Clement
Indexer: John Jefferson
Layout/Proofreading: Marie Kristine P. Leonardo, Gina Rexrode, Carrie Allen, Ellen Considine

Contents

Introduction

In today's fast-growing, ever-expanding, multi-cultural world the acquisition of at least one foreign language is a must for both business and pleasurable pursuits. If you're traveling, working, or just a student at heart, you may want or need an intensive crash course or a simple brush-up in French. The time to do it is NOW!

Learning French will allow you to enter a world of endless opportunities, intriguing experiences, and exciting challenges. Learning French will provide you with the key that opens the door to a different lifestyle, a distinctive culture, and a unique, romantic outlook on life. Learning French will give you a valuable tool that will serve you well when you least expect it. Open up your mind and immerse yourself in this wonderful experience. Study French with patience and love and the rewards you reap will be boundless.

What's on the Inside

So you're curious about French and that's why you've picked up this book! Learning this popular romance language is a very practical thing to do because it's used internationally: It's spoken on all seven continents throughout the world. Wherever your travels may take you, you'll find that a knowledge of French will prove invaluable and will greatly enrich your experiences.

Now if you're like most of us, you want to achieve quick and easy results with a minimum amount of work. Well, then this is the book for you. You'll painlessly and effortlessly learn all about pronunciation and grammar without having to sacrifice speed and accuracy. Students, travelers, and business people alike will find all the basics, in addition to common daily vocabulary and expressions that are useful in every conceivable situation. A wide range of top-ics is presented: food, clothing, health, leisure activities, business terms, and much more.

This book is not a phrase book, a travel guide, or a foreign language text. All of those are very task-specific. What makes *The Pocket Idiot's Guide to French* unique is that it compactly combines all three of these elements: It gives those who want an extremely good working command of French an extremely useful tool. In no time flat, you'll understand and be understood in French with ease and enjoyment. There'll be no embarrassment and no frustra-tion. Yes, learning French can be fun!

Extras to Help You Along

Besides the idiomatic expressions, helpful phrases, lists of vocabulary words, and down-to-earth grammar, this book has useful information provided in sidebars throughout the text. These elements are distinguished by the following icons:

Full Speed Ahead

A Full Speed Ahead box tells you how to work with French grammar easily, or reminds you of rules you might have forgotten from previous chapters.

Attention!

An Attention! tells you how to avoid making a mistake.

An Extra Workout

An Extra Workout gives you a chance to practice what you've learned. These tips will help you begin to put your French skills to use.

Acknowledgments

Thank you! Thank you! Thank you to some very special people who have made a difference in my life and have greatly enriched it.

A special: "I love you!," accompanied by hugs and kisses to:

Ray Elias for getting my program up and running, for ensuring that the local bookstores keep Stein in stock, and for being an even greater guy 38 years later; **Werner Elias** for making a very important delivery, for which I will be eternally grateful; **Roger H. Herz** for being a dear friend and a cooperative consultant; **Marty Hyman** for giving me the best legal advice imaginable; **Marty Leder** for making me laugh and keeping my spirits up; **Chris Levy** for being the best advisor and confidante in the world, for always knowing the right thing to do, and for teaching me lessons I needed to learn.

I would also like to acknowledge the contributions, input, support, and interest of the following people:

Natercia Alves, Marie-Claire Antoine, Monika Bergenthal, Vivian Bergenthal, Richard Calcasola of Maximus Hair Salon, Nancy Chu, Trudy Edelman, Richard Edelman, Barbara Gilson, Robert Grandt, François Haas of the Office of the French Treasury, Nancy Lasker of L'Oréal, Max Rechtman, Marie-Madeleine Saphire, and Barbara Shevrin.

Dedication

This book is dedicated to my patient, proofreader husband, Douglas; my skilled computer consultant son, Eric; my most ardent fan and son, Michael; to my parents, Sara and Jack Bernstein, whose love and support have helped me to become the woman I am today; and to my sister, Susan Opperman, who got all the art genes, my brother-in-law, Jay, who makes sure I stay warm, and Zachary, my precocious nephew.

The Quickest and Easiest Pronunciation Guide

It's really quite simple to sound irresistibly French especially if you were lucky enough to have been born with
a "good ear." If you can carry a tune or play a musical
instrument you should have no trouble at all imitating
the lilt, intonation, and stress of the language. Just follow
these fast and easy steps:

➤ Lose your inhibitions immediately and put on your
  best French accent. Don't be afraid to ham it up!

➤ Allow yourself to slip and slide the sounds together
  while speaking the language.

➤ Use your nose wisely for the correct pronunciation
  of French nasal sounds.

➤ Remember that some French accents change the
  sound of the letter on which they appear.

➤ Understand that practice and devotion will help
  improve your accent. Be patient!

Stress

In French, each syllable of a word has just about equal stress, so when speaking, try to pronounce each syllable of a word with equal emphasis. When you remember, place a slightly stronger emphasis on the last syllable of a group of words. Speak smoothly, speak musically, and speak evenly. My best advice: For maximum results, stay on an even keel.

A Liaison or an Elision?

Liaison (linking) and *elision* (sliding) are two linguistic elements of the French language that give it its fluidity and melodious beauty.

Liaison refers to the linking of the final consonant of one word with the beginning vowel of the next word.

Attention!

The one thing that you really want to avoid is overstress. Do not overemphasize letters, words, or syllables. This will target you as a novice and will ruin the sounds of the language.

Words	Liaison
Vous arrivez	*voo zah-ree-vay*

Elision occurs when there are two pronounced vowel sounds: one at the end of a word, and the other at the beginning of the next word. The first vowel is dropped and replaced by an apostrophe. Simply slide the words together:

Words	Elision	Pronunciation
Je + arrive	J'arrive	*zah-reev*
le + hôtel	l'hôtel	*lo-tehl*

Accent Marks

Think of accent marks as pronunciation guideposts that will help you speak like an old pro. There are five different accent marks in French that may be used to change the sounds of letters (*é* versus *è*, *a* versus *â*, and so on), to differentiate between the meanings of two words whose spellings are otherwise the same (*a* meaning "has" versus *à* meaning "to" or "at," *ou* meaning "or" versus *où* meaning "where," and so on), or to replace an *s* that was part of the word many centuries ago in old French.

➤ An *accent aigu* (´) is seen only on an *e* (é).

   é produces the sound (*ay*), as in *day*.

➤ An *accent grave* (`) is used with *a* (à), *e* (è), and *u* (ù).

   On an *e*, an accent grave produces the sound of (*eh*) as the *e* in the English word *met*. It doesn't change the sound of the *a* (à) or *u* (ù).

➤ An accent *circonflexe* (^) may be used on all vowels: *â, ê, î, ô, û*. The vowel sounds are longer for *â* and *ô*, are slightly longer for *ê*, and are imperceptible on *î* and *û*.

➤ A *cédille* (ç) is used only on a *c* (ç). When the *c* comes before *a, o,* or *u*, it means that you pronounce the letter as a soft *c* (the sound of *s*).

➤ A *tréma* (¨) occurs on a second vowel in a series. This accent indicates that the two vowels are pronounced separately, each having its own distinct sound: Haïti (*ay-ee-tee*), Noël (*noh-ehl*).

Many Vowel Sounds!

French vowels are a bit complicated because each one has a number of different sounds, and there are specific rules and accent marks that help you determine how the vowel should be pronounced.

The *é* may replace an *s* that used to exist in the word in old French. Adding a mental *s* immediately after *é* may enable you to easily determine the meaning of a word. See if the meaning jumps out at you: *éponge* (as in *sponge*), *étranger* (as in *stranger*)

This circumflex also often replaces an *s* from old French. Simply stick a mental *s* in the word to see if the meaning jumps out at you: *arrêter* (as in *arrest*), *fête* (as in *feast, festival*).

French Letter	Symbol	Pronunciation Guide
a, à, â	ah	Say **a** as in spa. Open wide and say ahhh…
é, final **er**, and **ez**; es in some words; a few ai, one-syllable et combinations é, final **er**, and **ez** are always pronounced **ay**.	ay	Say **ay** as in day.
e in one-syllable words or in the middle of a word followed by a single consonant	uh	Say **e** as in the.
è, ê, and e (plus two consonants or a final pronounced consonant) et, ei, ai	eh	Say **e** as in met.
i, î, y, ui	ee	Say **i** as in magazine.

French Letter	Symbol	Pronunciation Guide
i + ll il when preceded by a vowel	y	Say y as in your. For the ill, ail, or eil combinations, remember to keep the l silent.
i + ll in these words only	eel	Say the word **eel**.

Every rule has an exception; or in this case, because there aren't too many, the words might be worth memorizing—especially because they're used frequently.

ville *(veel)*   million *(mee-lyohN)*

village *(vee-lahzh)*   tranquille *(trahN-keel)*

mille *(meel)*

French Letter	Symbol	Pronunciation Guide
o (before se), o (last pronounced sound of word), ô, au, eau	o	Say o as in no. Keep your lips rounded.
o when followed by a pronounced consonant other than s	oh	Say o as in love.
ou, où, oû	oo	Say oo as in tooth.
oy, oi	wah	Say w as in watch.

You may be tempted to pronounce *oi* like *oy*, as the sound heard at the beginning of the word *oyster*. Avoid the pitfall. Practice the correct *wa* sound until you get it down pat.

French Letter	Symbol	Pronunciation Guide
u, û	ew	No equivalent

There really is no English sound equivalent to the French *u* sound. Try the following: Say the sound *oo* as in *Sue* while trying to say *ee* as in *see*. As you try to make the sound, concentrate on puckering your lips as if you just ate a very sour pickle. That's about as close as you can get.

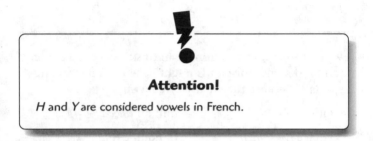

Attention!

H and *Y* are considered vowels in French.

The Nose Knows

Nasal sounds will occur when a vowel is followed by a single *N* or *M* in the same syllable. In the pronunciation guide, you will see a vowel sound followed by *N*. This indicates that you must make a nasal sound.

French Nasal	Symbol	Pronunciation Guide
an (am), en (em)	ahN	Similar to *on* with little emphasis on *n* Now hold your nose, say *on*.
in (im), ain (aim)	aN	Similar to *an* with little emphasis on *n*
oin	waN	Similar to *wa* of *wag*
ien	yaN	Similar to *yan* of *Yankee*
on (om)	ohN	Similar to *on* as in *long*
un (um)	uhN	Similar to *un* as in *under*

Concentrate on Consonants

Most final consonants are not pronounced except for final *c*, *r*, *f*, and *l* (think of the word *careful*). Final *s* is not pronounced in French, so avoid the temptation. Doing so will quickly unveil your amateur status.

French Letter	Symbol	Pronunciation Guide
b, d, f, k, l, m, n, p, s, t, v, z	The same	Same as English
c (hard sound before a, o, u, or consonant) qu, final q	k	Say the c as in card.
c (soft sound before e, i, y), ç, s at beginning of word, s next to a consonant, tion (t), x (only in the words given)	s	Say the c as in cent.
ch	sh	Say the ch as in machine.
g (hard sound before a, o, u, or consonant), gu (before i, e, y)	g	Say the g as in good.
g (soft sound before e, i, y), ge (soft before a, o), j	zh	Say the s as in pleasure.
gn	ny	Say the n as in union.
h		Always silent

Most of the time, *h* is used as a vowel and, therefore, requires elision with a vowel that might precede it: *l'homme* (*the man*). In other instances, *h* is used as a consonant and does not require elision with the preceding vowel: *le héros*. To tell how *h* is being used, you must look in a dictionary, where the consonant *h* is usually indicated with an *.

French Letter	Symbol	Pronunciation Guide
r	r	No equivalent

An Extra Workout

The French *r* requires the participation of your throat. First, drop your tongue to the bottom of your mouth and rest it against your teeth. Keep it out pressed there, out of your way. Now clear your throat or gargle and say "r" at the back of your throat at the same time. That's it—you've got the French *r*. A few words of advice: Do not roll your *r*; that's what they do in Spanish. Do not roll your tongue; that's what we do in English.

French Letter	Symbol	Pronunciation Guide
s (between vowels), sion	z	Say z as in zero.
th	t	Say t as in to. There is no th sound in French.
x	ks	Say xc as in excel.

Chapter 1

Strategies for Success

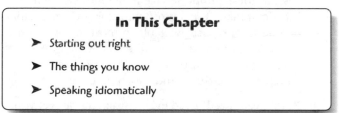

In This Chapter

➤ Starting out right

➤ The things you know

➤ Speaking idiomatically

So you've decided to learn French and you want to get off to a running start. Now you're looking for an uncomplicated but efficient way to accomplish this goal. It's simple: Just jump right in. That's right. Totally immerse yourself in anything and everything French. You have to have *une affaire d'amour* with the language, the culture, and the customs of the francophone world. If you want the key to a long-lasting, fulfilling, delightful relationship with French, just follow these tried and true suggestions:

➤ Examine your goals honestly. Assess your linguistic and auditory abilities. Decide how much time and energy you're willing to invest in your studies and then stick to your game plan. There's no hurry! Proceed at the pace that suits your needs.

➤ Make sure to invest in a good bilingual dictionary. Pocket varieties (which generally cost between $8 and $18) are more than sufficient for many learners. For the more serious-minded, however, a larger, more in-depth may prove necessary. Among the more popular, easy-to-use, comprehensive dictionaries, with a wide range of up-to-the-minute, colloquial, and idiomatic words and expressions are *Collins-Robert* (approximately $35) and *Larousse* (approximately $60).

➤ Never pass up an opportunity to become involved in the language. A wide variety of French films is available at large video stores (don't cheat and read the subtitles), public service radio and television broadcast many French programs, French magazines and newspapers are available in most major American cities. Look and listen all the time! Borrow language tapes from you local library or college and concentrate on the sounds of French.

➤ Read! Read! Read! Read everything you can get your hands on. Read to yourself, or out loud in front of a mirror, or to your good friends. It's easy to practice your comprehension and your accent all at once. Try comic books, children's books, and fairy tales. They're fun and entertaining! Pick up a copy of *Le Monde*, a French newspaper, and focus on what's happening in the francophone world.

➤ Find the most comfortable, learning-centered spot in your home and set up *un coin français* (a French corner). Use posters and articles to decorate this spot that will, from now on, be dedicated to your new project. Hang labeled pictures of vocabulary items you want to master. Organize and keep your French materials in this special area.

It's Time to Begin

Don't get nervous, but here's a quick pop quiz to see how much you know. Do you recognize: café, restaurant, amateur, boutique, bureau? Of course you do. Your knowledge of French is undoubtedly surprisingly extensive. You probably don't even realize just how many French words and expressions are already part of your vocabulary. And there are loads of phrases so similar to English, that you will find them very easy to use and understand with a minimal amount of effort.

Creating with Cognates

Want to develop a rather extensive French vocabulary in no time flat? It's a piece of cake! Just learn those cognates! What's a cognate? Quite simply it's a word that is spelled exactly the same, or almost the same, as a word in English and that has the same meaning. Sometimes we've actually borrowed the word from French, letter for letter, and have made it a part of our own vocabulary. Sure, cognates are pronounced differently in each language, but the meaning of the French word is quite obvious to anyone who speaks English.

An Extra Workout

Keep an alphabetical index card file of all the French cognates you know. Practice using them in sentences as often as you can. Use your best French accent to pronounce them.

Tables 1.1 and 1.2 will help you get a jump start on your list. They provide lists of words that are the same (or almost the same) in both languages:

Table 1.1 Perfect Cognates

Adjectives	Nouns		
	Le	**La**	**L'**
blond *blohN*	ballet *bah-leh*	blouse *blooz*	accident *ahk-see-dahN*
certain *sehr-taN*	bureau *bew-ro*	date *daht*	accord *ah-kohr*
content *kohN-tahN*	chef *shehf*	dispute *dees-pewt*	ambulance *ahN-bew-lahNs*
immense *ee-mahNs*	client *klee-yahN*	note *noht*	animal *ah-nee-mahl*
orange *oh-rahnzh*	hamburger *ahm-bewr-gehr*	photo *foh-to*	olive *oh-leev*
permanent *pehr-mah-nahN*	sandwich *sahNd-weesh*	route *root*	omelette *ohm-leht*
possible *poh-seebl*	soda *soh-dah*	table *tahbl*	orange *oh-rahnzh*

Full Speed Ahead

In French all nouns have a gender: either masculine or feminine. Use *le* to express *the* before a masculine singular noun, use *la* to express *the* before a feminine singular noun, use *l'* to express *the* before any singular noun that begins with a vowel.

Near Cognates

Table 1.2 lists the cognates that are nearly the same in both French and English. Take your time pronouncing the French words and compare them to their English equivalents. Remember: Your goal is to sound French.

Table 1.2   Almost Perfect Cognates

Adjectives	Nouns		
	Le	La	L'
américain *ah-may-ree-kaN*	bébé *bay-bay*	banque *buhNk*	acteur *ahk-tuhr*
amusant *ah-mew-zahN*	dictionnaire *deek-syoh-nehr*	cathédrale *kah-tay-drahl*	adresse *ah-drehs*
bleu *bluh*	dîner *dee-nay*	couleur *koo-luhr*	âge *ahzh*
confortable *kohN fohr-tabl*	docteur *dohk-tuhr*	famille *fah-mee-y*	agence *ah-zhahNs*
délicieux *day-lee-syuh*	papier *pah-pyay*	lampe *lahNp*	appartement *ah-pahr-tuh-mahN*
différent *dee-fay-rahN*	parc *pahrk*	lettre *lehtr*	artiste *ahr-teest*
élégant *ay-lay-gahN*	serveur *sehr-vuhr*	musique *mew-zeek*	exemple *ehks-zahNpl*
intéressant *aN-tay-reh-sahN*	téléphone *tay-lay-fohn*	pharmacie *fahr-mah-see*	hôtel *o-tehl*
populaire *poh-pew-lehr*	touriste *too-reest*	soupe *soop*	oncle *ohNkl*
riche *reesh*	vendeur *vahN-duhr*	télévision *tay-lay-vee-zyohN*	université *ew-nee-vehr-see-tay*

Verbs

Verbs (action words) can also be cognates. Most French verbs fall into one of three families: *-er* verbs, *-ir* verbs, and *-re* verbs. These verbs are considered regular because all verbs in the same family follow the same rules.

All French verbs must be conjugated. This means the verb form must have an ending that matches its subject. We do this automatically and naturally in English without giving it a moment's thought. It's not that difficult in French and you will be able to learn it quickly. Verb conjugation will be explained in greater detail in Chapter 2.

Of course you'll find these verb cognates a snap to recognize:

French	Pronunciation	French	Pronunciation
	The ER Family		
accompagner	*ah-kohN-pah-nyay*	observer	*ohb-sehr-vay*
adorer	*ah-doh-ray*	pardonner	*pahr-doh-nay*
aider	*eh-day*	passer	*pah-say*
changer	*shahN-zhay*	payer	*peh-yay*
commencer	*koh-mahN-say*	préparer	*pray-pah-ray*
danser	*dahN-say*	présenter	*pray-zahN-tay*
décider	*day-see-day*	recommander	*ruh-koh-mahN-day*
demander	*duh-mahN-day*	refuser	*ruh-few-zay*
désirer	*day-zee-ray*	regarder	*ruh-gahr-day*
dîner	*dee-nay*	regretter	*ruh-greh-tay*
entrer	*ahN-tray*	réparer	*ray-pah-ray*
hésiter	*ay-zee-tay*	réserver	*ray-zehr-vay*
ignorer	*ee-nyoh-ray*	signer	*see-nyay*
inviter	*aN-vee-tay*	tourner	*toor-nay*
The IR Family		*The RE Family*	
accomplir	*ah-kohN-pleer*	défendre	*day-fahNdr*
applaudir	*ah-plo-deer*	répondre	*ray-pohNdr*
finir	*fee-neer*	vendre	*vahNdr*

Watch out for words that look like cognates but have a different meaning:

attendre *(ah-tahNdr)*	to wait
comment *(koh-mahN)*	how
la librairie *(lah lee-breh-ree)*	bookstore
l'occasion *(loh-kah-zyohN)*	opportunity
le raisin *(luh reh-zaN)*	grape
rester *(rehs-tay)*	to remain
sale *(sahl)*	dirty
travailler *(trah-vah-yay)*	to work

Special Tricks

Some special tricks on pronunciation have already been mentioned. When you look at Table 1.3, you will see how adding an *s* after an accent circonflexe (^) and how substituting an *s* for an *é* or adding one after it will help you figure out the meanings of many words.

Table 1.3   Special Tricks

accent (^)	English	é	English
coûter *(koo-tay)*	to cost	écarlate *(ay-kahr-laht)*	scarlet
croûte *(kroot)*	crust	échapper *(ay-shah-pay)*	to escape
fête *(feht)*	feast	école *(ay kohl)*	school
forêt *(foh-reh)*	forest	épice *(ay-pees)*	spice
hôpital *(o-pee-tahl)*	hospital	éponge *(ay-pohNzh)*	sponge

Idiomatic French

What do we mean by an idiom? In any language, an *idiom* is a particular word or expression whose meaning cannot be readily understood by analyzing its traditional grammatical construction or its component words. Some common English idioms are:

You'll have to pay through the nose.

I have to buy some time.

She called his bluff.

Don't jump the gun.

All languages contain idiomatic expressions that must be memorized. That's why it's impossible to translate word for word from one language to another. A better idea is just try to think of the phrase you want in the language you want.

You will become better acquainted with many French idioms as you go from chapter to chapter.

An Extra Workout

Keep a file of index cards that contain the idioms you learn in each chapter. Try to use the ones that will be most useful to you in situations in which you will speak the language.

Chapter 2

Grammar in a Flash

In This Chapter

➤ Nouns

➤ Verbs

➤ Adjectives

➤ Adverbs

➤ Prepositions

So you really want to speak French like a native. Well, you'll be delighted to know that speaking a foreign language doesn't mean that you have to spend hours memorizing pages of rules and translating sentences word for word. That's the way it was done in school years ago. Many of us can remember that drudgery. With today's new communicative approach, however, it's totally unnecessary for to walk around armed with a cumbersome French dictionary. Students are now encouraged to use the language and its patterns naturally, the way a native speaker does. To achieve this goal, you need to know some basic grammar.

The Noun's the Thing

Nouns refer to people, places, things, or ideas. Just like in English, nouns can be replaced by pronouns (such as he, she, it, they). Unlike in English, however, all nouns in French have a gender. This means that all nouns have a *sex*. Now that I have your attention I hate to disappoint you. In this case, *sex* refers to the masculine or feminine designation of the noun. In French, all nouns also have a number (singular or plural). Short articles (words that stand for "the" or "a") serve as noun identifiers and usually help to indicate gender and number. Don't be overly concerned by this. Even if you use the incorrect gender or number, you'll still be understood as long as you select the appropriate word.

Attention!

Beware of trying to use your common sense to guess gender: makeup, stockings, and pocketbook are masculine, while car, shirt, and fishing are feminine.

Gender

Gender, of course, is very obvious if you're speaking about a man or a woman. But it can be a little tricky with all those other nouns that refer to objects. Use the noun identifiers in Table 2.1 to express "the" or "a":

Table 2.1 Singular Noun Markers

	Masculine	Feminine
the	le (l') (*luh*)	la (l') (*lah*)
a, an, one	un (*uhN*)	une (*ewn*)

Attention!

The definite articles *le* and *la* become *l'* for words beginning with a vowel or vowel sound (*h, y*). Although it's quite easy to determine the masculine or feminine gender of the noun when *le* or *la* is used, the noun's gender remains a mystery when *l'* (masculine or feminine) is used. To speak properly, you'll have to learn the indefinite article *un* or *une* for any word that begins with a vowel.

Some nouns can be either masculine or feminine depending on whether the speaker is referring to a male or female. Just change the article without changing the spelling of the noun:

un enfant   une enfant

le touriste   la touriste

Some nouns are always only masculine or feminine no matter the sex of the person to whom you are referring:

Always Masculine	Always Feminine
bébé (*bay-bay*)/baby	acquaintance (*koh-neh-sahNs*)/ connaissance
dentiste (*dahN-teest*)/dentist	personne (*pehr-sohn*)/person
médecin (*mayd-saN*)/doctor	vedette (*vuh-deht*)/star
professeur (*proh-feh-suhr*)/teacher	victime (*veek-teem*)/victim

Some noun endings can really make the job of determining gender quite easy. Table 2.2 provides a list of endings that will help do this:

Table 2.2   Masculine and Feminine Endings

Masculine Ending	Example	Feminine Ending	Example
-acle	spectacle (*spehk-tahkl*)	-ade	limonade (*lee-moh-nahd*)
-age*	garage (*gah-rahzh*)	-ale	cathédrale (*kah-tay-drahl*)
-al	animal (*ah-nee-mahl*)	-ance	chance (*shahNs*)
-eau**	château (*shah-to*)	-ence	essence (*eh-sahNs*)
-et	ticket (*tee-keh*)	-ette	chaînette (*sheh-neht*)
-ier	papier (*pah-pyay*)	-ie	magie (*mah-zhee*)
-isme	cyclisme (*see-kleez-muh*)	-ique	boutique (*boo-teek*)
-ment	changement (*shahNzh-mahN*)	-oire	histoire (*ees-twahr*)
		-sion	expression (*ehks-preh-syohN*)
		-tion	addition (*ah-dee-syohN*)
		-ure	coiffure (*kwah-fewr*)

* except page (pahzh) (f.); plage (plahzh) (f.) beach
** except eau (o) (f.) water; peau (po) (f.) skin

A fast and simple way to get the feminine form of some nouns is to add an *e* to the masculine form. This will create a change in the pronunciation of any feminine noun ending in a *consonant + e*. For the masculine noun, the final consonant is not pronounced. For the feminine, the consonant must then be pronounced. Another change is that the final nasal sound of a masculine *in* (*aN*) ending loses its nasality when the feminine ending becomes *ine* (*een*). These changes appear in Table 2.3.

Attention!

The *e* is never dropped from the indefinite article *une*. The final *e* does, however, change the sound of the word *un* (*uhN*) to *une* (*ewn*).

Table 2.3   Gender Changes

Le (L'), Un	La (L'), Une
ami (*ah-mee*)/friend	amie (*ah-mee*)/friend
avocat (*ah-vo-kah*)/lawyer	avocate (*ah-vo-kaht*)/lawyer
client (*klee-yahN*)/client	cliente (*klee-yahNt*)/client
cousin (*koo-zaN*)/cousin	cousine (*koo-zeen*)/cousin

Some masculine noun endings (usually referring to professions) very conveniently have a corresponding feminine ending. Most of the feminine endings sound different, as you will notice in Table 2.4.

Table 2.4 More Sex Changes

Masculine/ Feminine Ending	Example
-an	paysan (*peh-ee-zahN*)/peasant
-anne	paysanne (*peh-ee-zahn*)/peasant
-er	épicier (*ay-pee-syay*)/grocer
-ère	épicière (*ay-pee-syehr*)/grocer
-eur	programmeur(*proh-grah-muhr*)/programmer
-euse	programmeuse/(*proh-grah-muhz*)/programmer
-ien	pharmacien(*fahr-mah-syaN*)/pharmacist
-ienne	pharmacienne/(fahr-mah-*syehn*)pharmacist
-on	patron (*pah-trohN*)/boss
-onne	patronne (*pah-trohn*)/boss
-teur	acteur (*ahk-tuhr*)/actor
-trice	arice (*ahk -trees*)/actrice

Don't use the article *un* or *une* before the name of a profession:

Il est dentiste.   Elle est avocate.

Number

If a French noun refers to more than one person, place, thing, or idea, just like in English, it can be made plural. Table 2.5 shows that it is not enough to simply change the noun. The identifying article must be made plural as well:

Table 2.5 Plural Noun Markers

	Masculine	Feminine
the	les	les
some	des	des

As you see, since plural noun markers are used for both feminine and masculine nouns, they do not enable you to determine gender. They indicate only that the speaker is referring to more than one noun. This means that you must learn each noun with its singular noun marker.

Plural Nouns

It's really quite easy to form the plural of most nouns in French. Just add an *unpronounced s* to the singular form:

le garçon (*luh gahr-sohN*),   les garçons (*lay gahr-sohN*),
un garçon (*uhN gahr-sohN*)   des garçons (*day gahr-sohN*)

la fille (*lah fee-y*),   les filles (*lay fee-y*),
une fille (*ewn fee-y*)   des filles (*day fee-y*)

l'enfant (*lahN-fahN*),   les enfants (*lay zahN-fahN*),
un enfant   des enfants (*day zahN-fahN*)
(*uhN nahN-fahN*)

The French also use the letters *s*, *x*, and *z* to make plurals. What happens if you have a French noun that ends in one of these letters? Absolutely nothing!

le prix (*luh pree*)/   les prix (*lay pree*)
the price, prize

le fils (*luh fees*)/ the son   les fils (*lay fees*)

Common words that end in *s:*

l'autobus (*lo-toh-bews*)/bus   le mois (*luh mwah*)/month

le bras (*luh brah*)/arm   le pays (*luh pay-ee*)/country

la fois (*lah fwah*)/time   le repas (*luh ruh-pah*)/meal

Common words that end in *x:*

la croix (*lah krwah*)/   la voix (*lah vwah*)/voice
cross

Other Plurals

The letter *x* is used in French to make plurals.

➤ For nouns ending in *eau:*

le bateau (*luh bah-to*)/boat   les bateaux

➤ For nouns ending in *eu,* except *le pneu* (*luh pnuh*)/ tire: *les pneus:*

le cheveu (*luh shuh vuh*)/hair   les cheveux

➤ For nouns ending in *al,* change *al* to *aux* except for le bal (*luh bahl*)/ball: bals; le festival (*luh fehs-tee-vahl*)/festival: festivals:

l'animal   les animaux
(*lah nee mahl*)/animal

➤ For some nouns ending in *ou,* add *x* to form the plural:

le bijou   les bijoux
(*luh bee-zhoo*)/jewel

➤ Just as we have some words in English that are always plural (pants, sunglasses, shorts, news), so do the French. Here are some nouns that might prove useful to you:

les ciseaux (m.)   les lunettes (f.)
(*lay see-zo*)/ scissors   (*lay lew-neht*)/eyeglasses

les gens (m.)   les vacances (f.)
(*lay zhahN*)/people   (*lay vah-kahNs*)/vacation

Verbs Show Action

Verbs indicate an action or a state of being. All verbs must have a subject, whether it is expressed in a statement or implied in a command. The subject can be a noun or pronoun, and, just like in English, it is given a person and a number as shown in Table 2.6:

Table 2.6 Subject Pronouns

Person	Singular		Plural	
first	je* (*zhuh*)	I	nous (*noo*)	we
second	tu** (*tew*)	you	vous** (*voo*)	you
third	il (*eel*)	he, it	ils*** (*eel*)	they
	elle (*ehl*)	she, it	elles (*ehl*)	they
	on (*ohN*)	one, you, we, they		

*The subject pronoun je requires elision and becomes j' before a vowel or vowel sound (h, y).

**The subject pronoun tu is used when speaking to a single (one) friend, relative, child, or pet. Tu is called the familiar form. The u from tu is never dropped for elision: tu arrives.

**The subject pronoun vous is used in the singular to show respect to an older person or when speaking to someone you don't know very well. Vous is always used when speaking to more than one person, regardless of familiarity. Vous is referred to as the polite form.

***The subject pronoun ils is used to refer to more than one male or a combined group of males and females.

Regular Verbs

Verbs are shown in their infinitive form: *to* live, *to* laugh, *to* love. An infinitive is the form of the verb before it has been conjugated. In a normal English conversation, we conjugate verbs automatically without even paying attention to what we're doing. *Conjugation* refers to changing the ending of a verb so it agrees with the subject. Verbs can be regular (they follow a set pattern of rules) or irregular (there are no rules so you must memorize them).

There are three large families of regular verbs in French: verbs whose infinitives end in er, ir, or re. The verbs within each family are all conjugated in exactly the same manner, so after you've learned the pattern for one family, you know all the verbs in that family. Just drop the underlined infinitive endings and add the conjugated ending that corresponds to the subject:

trouv<u>er</u> (to find)	chois<u>ir</u> (to choose)	attend<u>re</u> (to wait)
je trouve *zhuh troov*	je choisis *zhuh shwah-zee*	j'attends *zhah-tahN*
tu trouves *tew troov*	tu choisis *tew shwah-zee*	tu attends *tew ah-tahN*
il, elle, on trouve *eel, ehl, ohN troov*	il, elle, on choisit *eel, ehl, ohN shwah-zee*	il, elle, on attend *eel, ehl, ohN nah-tahN*
nous trouvons *noo troo-vohN*	nous choisissons *noo shwah-zee-sohN*	nous attendons *noo zah-tahN-dohN*
vous trouvez *voo troo-vay*	vous choisissez *voo shwah-zee-say*	vous attendez *voo zah-tahN-day*
ils, elles trouvent *eel, ehl troov*	ils, elles choisissent *eel, ehl shwah-zees*	ils, elles attendent *eel, ehl zah-tahN*

An Extra Workout

If you want to increase your vocabulary quickly, you should have as many verbs as you can on the tip of your tongue. Paste the verb tables below to your refrigerator. Every time you stop for a drink or a snack, choose five new verbs to memorize.

Verb Tables

Tables 2.7, 2.8, and 2.9 provide practical lists of the most frequently used regular verbs in all three families. These are the ones you'll use the most in any given situation:

Table 2.7 Common –er Verbs

French	English	French	English
aider (*eh-day*)	to help	chercher (*shehr-shay*)	to look for
commencer (*koh-mahN-say*)	to begin	demander (*duh-mahN-day*)	to ask
dépenser (*day-pahN-say*)	to spend (money)	donner (*doh-nay*)	to give
écouter (*ay-koo-tay*)	to listen (to)	étudier (*ay-tew-dyay*)	to study
fermer (*fehr-may*)	to close	habiter (*ah-bee-tay*)	to live (in)
jouer (*zhoo-ay*)	to play	oublier (*oo-blee-yay*)	to forget
manger (*mahN-zhay*)	to eat	parler (*pahr-lay*)	to speak
penser (*pahN-say*)	to think	préparer (*pray-pah-ray*)	to prepare
présenter (*pray-zahN-tay*)	to present, introduce	regarder (*ruh-gahr-day*)	to look at, watch
rencontrer (*rahN-kohN-tray*)	to meet	signer (*see-nyay*)	to sign
téléphoner (*tay-lay-foh-nay*)	to telephone	travailler (*trah-vah-yay*)	to work
voyager (*vwah-yah-zhay*)	to travel		

Table 2.8 Common –ir Verbs

French	Pronunciation	English
choisir	*shwah-zeer*	to choose
finir	*fee-neer*	to finish
guérir	*gay-reer*	to cure
jouir	*zhoo-eer*	to enjoy
réfléchir	*ray-flay-sheer*	to reflect, think
réussir	*ray-ew-seer*	to succeed

Table 2.9   Common –re Verbs

French	Pronunciation	English
attendre	*ah-tahNdr*	to wait (for)
descendre	*deh-sahNdr*	to go (come) down
entendre	*ahN-tahNdr*	to hear
perdre	*pehrdr*	to lose
répondre	*ray-pohNdr ah*	to answer
vendre	*vahNdr*	to sell

All About Adjectives

Adjectives are used to describe nouns. All French adjectives must agree in number and gender with the nouns they modify. In a French sentence, all words must agree with each other. In other words, if a noun is plural, its adjective must also be plural. And if the noun is feminine, you must be careful to use the feminine form of the adjective.

An Extra Workout

Describe your family members and friends using the adjectives given in the tables below. Select a different person every day and use as many adjectives as you can to describe him or her.

You can easily form the feminine of most adjectives by adding an *e* to the masculine form as shown in Table 2.10:

Table 2.10   Forming Feminine Adjectives

Masculine		Feminine		Meaning
âgé	*ah-zhay*	âgée	*ah-zhay*	old, aged
américain	*ah-may-ree-kahN*	américaine	*ah-may-ree-kehn*	American
amusant	*ah-mew-zahN*	amusante	*ah-mew-zahNt*	amusing, fun
blond	*blohN*	blonde	*blohNd*	blond
charmant	*shahr-mahN*	charmante	*shahr-mahNt*	charming
content	*kohN-tahN*	contente	*kohN-tahNt*	glad
élégant	*ay-lay-gahN*	élégante	*ay-lay-gahNt*	elegant
fort	*fohr*	forte	*fohrt*	strong
français	*frahN-seh*	française	*frahN-sehz*	French
grand	*grahN*	grande	*grahNd*	big
intelligent	*aN-teh-lee-zhahN*	intelligente	*aN-teh-lee-zhahNt*	intelligent
joli	*zhoh-lee*	jolie	*zhoh-lee*	pretty
petit	*puh-tee*	petite	*puh-teet*	small
poli	*poh-lee*	polie	*poh-lee*	polite

When an adjective ends in an *e* in its masculine form, it is not necessary to make any changes at all to get the feminine form. Both are spelled and pronounced exactly the same:

cé|èbre (*say-lehbr*)/famous   mince (*maNs*)/thin

comique (*koh-meek*)/comical   propre (*prohpr*/clean

facile (*fah-seel*)/easy   sale (*sahl*)/dirty

honnête (*oh-neht*)/honest   triste (*treest*)/sad

When a masculine adjective ends in *x*, the feminine is formed by changing *x* to *se*, which gives the feminine ending a *z* sound, as seen in Table 2.11:

Table 2.11 Adjectives Ending in eux and euse

Masculine		Feminine	
affectueux	*ah-fehk-tew-uh*	affectueuse	*ah-fehk-tew-uhz*
ambitieux	*ahN-bee-syuh*	ambitieuse	*ahN-bee-syuhz*
délicieux	*day-lee-syuh*	délicieuse	*day-lee-syuhz*
généreux	*zhay-nay-ruh*	généreuse	*zhay-nay-ruhz*
heureux (happy)	*uh-ruh*	heureuse	*uh-ruhz*
sérieux	*say-ryuh*	sérieuse	*say-ryuhz*

When a masculine adjective ends in *f,* the feminine is formed by changing *f* to *ve.* See Table 2.12 for pronunciation changes.

Table 2.12 Adjectives Ending in f and ve

Masculine		Feminine	
actif	*ahk-teef*	active	*ahk-teev*
attentif	*ah-tahN-teef*	attentive	*ah-tahN-teev*
imaginatif	*ee-mah-zhee-nah-teef*	imaginative	*ee-mah-zhee-nah-teev*
naïf	*nah-eef*	naïve	*nah-eev*
sportif	*spohr-teef*	sportive	*spohr-teev*

When a masculine adjective ends in *er,* the feminine is formed by changing *er* to *ère,* as shown in Table 2.13:

Table 2.13 Adjectives Ending in er and ère

Masculine		Feminine		Meaning
cher	*shehr*	chère	*shehr*	dear, expensive
dernier	*dehr-nyay*	dernière	*dehr-nyehr*	last
étranger	*ay-trahN-zhay*	étrangère	*ay-trahN-zhehr*	foreign

Masculine		Feminine		Meaning
fier	*fyehr*	fière	*fyehr*	proud
premier	*pruh-myay*	première	*puh-myehr*	first

Some masculine adjectives double the final consonant and then add *e* to form the feminine, as shown in Table 2.14.

Table 2.14 Adjectives that Double Their Consonants

Masculine		Feminine		Meaning
ancien	*ahN-syaN*	ancienne	*ahN-syehn*	ancient, old
bas	*bah*	basse	*bahs*	low
bon	*bohN*	bonne	*bohn*	good
européen	*ew-roh-pay-aN*	européenne	*ew-roh-pay-ehn*	European
gentil	*zhahN-tee-y*	gentille	*zhahN-tee-y*	nice, kind
gros	*gro*	grosse	*gros*	fat, big
mignon	*mee-nyohN*	mignonne	*mee-noyhn*	cute

Finally, the adjectives in Table 2.15 list irregular feminine forms that must be memorized.

Table 2.15 Irregular Adjectives

Masculine		Feminine		Meaning
beau*	*bo*	belle	*behl*	beautiful
blanc	*blahN*	blanche	*blahNsh*	white
complet	*kohN-pleh*	complète	*kohN-pleht*	complete
doux	*doo*	douce	*doos*	sweet, gentle
faux	*fo*	fausse	*fos*	false
favori	*fah-voh-ree*	favorite	*fah-voh-reet*	favorite

continues

Table 2.15 Continued

Masculine		Feminine		Meaning
frais	*freh*	fraîche	*frehsh*	fresh
long	*lohN*	longue	*lohNg*	long
nouveau*	*noo-vo*	nouvelle	*noo-vehl*	new
vieux*	*vyuh*	vieille	*vyay*	old

*The French use special forms: bel, nouvel, and vieil **before** masculine nouns beginning with a vowel or vowel sound to prevent a clash between two pronounced vowel sounds. This allows the language to flow.*

   un bel appartement   un nouvel appartement
   un vieil appartement

*If the adjective comes **after** the noun, then the regular masculine form is used:*

L'appartement est beau.
L'appartement est nouveau.
L'appartement est vieux.

Making Adjectives Plural

Most adjectives are made plural by adding an unpronounced *s* to the singular form: timide(s), charmant(e)s, joli(e)s, fatigué(e)s.

If an adjective ends in *s* or *x*, it is unnecessary to add the *s:* exquis, heureux.

Most masculine singular adjectives ending in *al* change *al* to *aux* in the plural: spéciaux.

The special masculine singular adjectives *bel, nouvel,* and *vieil* do not need special plural forms, since the problem of having two conflicting vowels is eliminated with the *x* consonant sound of the plural ending.

Singular	Plural	Example
bel	beaux	de beaux appartements
nouvel	nouveaux	de nouveaux appartements
vieil	vieux	de vieux appartements

The masculine singular adjective tout (all) becomes tous in the plural.

The Position of Adjectives

In French, most adjectives are placed after the nouns they modify. Compare this with English, where we do the opposite:

un homme intéressant   an interesting man

Adjectives showing:

BEAUTY: beau, joli

AGE: jeune, nouveau, vieux

GOODNESS (or lack of it): bon, gentil, mauvais, vilain

SIZE: grand, petit, court, long, gros, large

generally go before the nouns they modify. Remember **BAGS**, and you'll have no trouble with these adjectives:

un beau garçon   a handsome boy

une large avenue   a wide avenue

If more than one adjective is being used in a description, put each adjective in its proper position:

une bonne histoire intéresante

une large et jolie avenue

un homme charmant et intelligent

Using Adverbs

How Well Do You Do Things?

Adverbs are words that describe verbs, adjectives, or other adverbs. In English, most adverbs end in -*ly:* for example, He dances slowly. In French, however, they end in -*ment:* for example, *Il dance lentement.* Adverbs shouldn't pose many problems as you learn the language.

Add *ment* to the masculine, singular form of adjectives that end in a vowel. If the masculine form of the adjective

ends in a consonant, first change it to the feminine form
and then add *ment*.

How to form adverbs using masculine adjectives:

Adjective	Adverb	Meaning
passionné (*pah-syoh-nay*)	passionnément (*pah-syoh-nay-mahN*)	enthusiastically
rapide (*rah-peed*)	rapidement (*rah-peed-mahN*)	rapidly, quickly
vrai (*vreh*)	vraiment (*vreh-mahN*)	truly, really

How to form adverbs from feminine adjectives:

Adjective	Adverb	Meaning
lente (*lahNt*)	lentement (*lahNt-mahN*)	slowly
seule (*suhl*)	seulement (*suhl-mahN*)	only
active (*ahk-teev*)	activement (*ahk-teev-mahN*)	actively
complète (*kohN-pleht*)	complètement (*kohN-pleht-mahN*)	completely
continuelle (*kohN-tee-new-ehl*)	continuellement (*kohN-tee-new-ehl-mahN*)	continuously
douce (*doos*)	doucement (*doos-mahN*)	gently
fière (*fyehr*)	fièrement (*fyehr-mahN*)	proudly
franche (*frahNsh*)	franchement (*frahNsh-mahN*)	frankly
sérieuse (*say-ree-uhz*)	sérieusement (*say-ree-uhz-mahN*)	seriously

Exceptions to the Rule

Wouldn't life be so easy if there were no exceptions to the
rules? Fortunately, the irregularities in French adverbs are
easy to understand and should present no difficulties.

Some adverbs are formed by changing a silent *e* from the
adjective to *é* before the adverbial *ment* ending:

Adjective	Adverb	Meaning
énorme (*ay-nohrm*)	énormément (*ay-nohr-may-mahN*)	enormously
profond (*proh-fohN*)	profondément (*proh-fohN-day-mahN*)	profoundly

Adjectives ending in *ant* and *ent* have adverbs ending in *amment* and *emment* respectively:

Adjective	Adverb	Meaning
constant (*kohN-stahN*)	constamment (*kohN-stah-mahN*)	constantly
courant (*koo-rahN*)	couramment (*koo-rah-mahN*)	fluently
évident (*ay-vee-dahN*)	évidemment (*ay-vee-deh-mahN*)	evidently
récent (*ray-sahN*)	récemment (*ray-seh-mahN*)	recently

Be careful with these adverbs that have distinct forms from adjectives:

Adjective	Adverb
bon (*bohN*)/good	bien (*byaN*)/well
mauvais (*moh-veh*)/bad	mal (*mahl*)/badly
meilleur (*meh-yuhr*)/better	mieux (*myuh*)/better
petit (*puh-tee*)/little	peu (*puh*)/little

If you can't think of the adverb, or if one does not exist, use the phrases d'une façon (*dewn fah-sohN*) or d'une manière (*dewn mah-nyehr*), which both express *in a way, in a manner,* or *in a fashion.*

He plays intelligently.
Il joue d'une façon (d'une manière) intelligent.

Some adverbs and adverbial expressions are not formed from adjectives at all and, therefore, do not end in *ment*. Table 2.16 gives the most common adverbs that follow this rule. These familiar, high-frequency words are extremely useful in everyday conversation.

Table 2.16 Adverbs not Formed from Adjectives

French	English	French	English
alors (*ah-lohrs*)	then	après (*ah-preh*)	afterward
aussi (*o-see*)	also, too	beaucoup (*bo-koo*)	much
bientôt (*byaN-to*)	soon	comme (*kohm*)	as
d'habitude (*dah-bee-tewd*)	usually, generally	déjà (*day-zhah*)	already
encore (*ahN-kohr*)	still, yet, again	ensemble (*ahN-sahNbl*)	together
maintenant (*maNt-nahN*)	now	moins (*mwaN*)	less
plus (*plew*)	more	quelquefois (*kehl-kuh-fwah*)	sometimes
souvent (*soo-vahN*)	often	tard (*tahr*)	late
tôt (*to*)	soon, early	toujours (*too-zhoor*)	always, still
tout (*too*)	quite, entirely	très (*treh*)	very
trop (*tro*)	too much	vite (*veet*)	quickly

Position of Adverbs

Adverbs are generally placed after the verb they modify. Sometimes, however, the position of the adverb is variable and is usually placed where we would logically put an English adverb.

D'habitude il joue bien au football.
Il joue très bien au football.

An Extra Workout

Make a list of five things you like to do and how well you do them. Practice reading your list aloud.

Prepositions

Prepositions show the relationship between a noun and another word in a sentence. Table 2.17 shows common prepositions you will find useful:

Table 2.17   Prepositions

French	English	French	English
à (*ah*)	to, at	après (*ah-preh*)	after
avant (*ah-vahN*)	before	chez (*shay*)	at the house (business) of
contre (*kohNtr*)	against	dans (*dahN*)	in
de (*duh*)	from	derrière (*deh-ryehr*)	behind
devant (*duh-vahN*)	in front of	en (*ahN*)	in
entre (*ahNtr*)	between	loin (de) (*lwaN*) (*duh*)	far (from)
par (*pahr*)	by, through	pour (*poor*)	for, in order to
près (de) (*preh*) (*duh*)	near	sans (*sahN*)	without
sous (*soo*)	under	sur (*sewr*)	on
vers (*vehr*)	toward		

The following pronouns are used after prepositions:

moi	me	nous	us
toi	you	vous	you
lui	him	eux	them (m.)
elle	her	elles	them (f.)

Chapter 3

YOU Are the Subject

moi ?

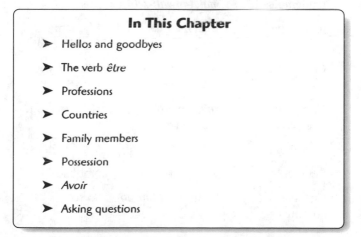

In This Chapter

➤ Hellos and goodbyes

➤ The verb *être*

➤ Professions

➤ Countries

➤ Family members

➤ Possession

➤ *Avoir*

➤ Asking questions

A foolproof way to quickly immerse yourself in French is to find a foreign friend with a sympathetic ear. Then just jabber away. Talk about anything and everything that interests you. Don't worry about your mistakes. A real friend will politely let you get away with the less severe ones. Don't be shy about asking for help and corrections. No one is perfect. By all means use your dictionary or ask for help when you get stuck. Developing a friendship requires you to talk about yourself and to ask your new-found friend questions. Start to strike up a conversation by using the phrases below as an opener:

Since you don't know the person at all, a formal approach is *de rigueur* (mandatory). A typical opening conversation might start with many of these phrases:

Bonjour	*bohN-zhoor*	Hello.
Bonsoir	*bohN swahr*	Good evening.
monsieur	*muh-syuh*	Sir
madame	*mah-dahm*	Miss, Mrs.
mademoiselle	*mahd-mwah-zehl*	Miss
Je m'appelle	*zhuh mah-pehl*	My name is (I call myself)
Comment vous appelez-vous?	*kohN-mahN voo zah-play voo*	What is your name?
Comment allez-vous?	*kohN-mahN tah-lay voo*	How are you?
Très bien.	*treh byaN*	Very well.
Pas mal.	*pah mahl*	Not bad.
Comme ci comme ça.	*kohm see kohm sah*	So so.

I Am What I Am

If you're like most people, you like to talk about yourself and also find out about others. Making the other person the center of attention is sure to win you friends. To ask and answer the simplest questions in French, you need to know the verb *être*—to be. This is your first irregular verb, so be prepared to memorize all its forms as shown in Table 3.1.

Table 3.1   The Verb être (to be)

French	Pronunciation	English
je suis	*zhuh swee*	I am
tu es	*tew eh*	you are
il, elle, on est	*eel (ehl) (ohN) eh*	he, she, one is
nous sommes	*noo sohm*	we are
vous êtes	*voo zeht*	you are
ils, elles sont	*eel (ehl) sohN*	they are

If you detect an unfamiliar accent when speaking to an acquaintance, get ready to satisfy your curiosity by using *être* to ask about a person's origins.

Vous êtes d'où?	*voo zeht doo*	Where are you from?
Je suis de ...(city).	*zhuh swee duh*	I am from ...(city).

To express the state you come from, keep the following in mind:

Use *de* (from) for all feminine states: any state ending in *e* and for any state whose name has an adjective:

> Je suis de Maine.

> Je suis de New York.

Use *du* (from) for all masculine states: sates ending in any letter other than *e*.

> Je suis du Vermont.

Use *des* (from) to say that you come from the U.S.

Je suis des États-Unis.

What's Your Line?

Use *être* to talk about your job or to ask about someone else's. The feminine forms are given in parentheses in Table 3.2.

Quel est votre mètier?	*kehl eh vohtr may-tyay*	What is your profession?

Attention!

Remember that some occupations have only masculine or feminine forms despite the gender of the person employed. Other professions use the same word for masculine and feminine employees.

Table 3.2 Professions

English	French	Pronunciation
accountant	comptable	*kohN-tahbl*
dentist	dentiste (m.)	*dahN-teest*
doctor	docteur (m.)	*dohk-tuhr*
hairdresser	coiffeur (coiffeuse)	*kwah-fuhr (kwah-fuhz)*
jeweler	bijoutier (bijoutière)	*bee-zhoo-tyay (bee-zhoo-tyehr)*
lawyer	avocat(e)	*ah-voh-kah(t)*
manager	gérant(e)	*zhay-rahN(t)*

English	French	Pronunciation
nurse	infirmier (infirmière)	*aN-feer-myay (ahN-feer-myehr)*
police officer	agent de police (m.)	*ah-zhahN duh poh-lees*
secretary	secrétaire (m. or f.)	*seh-kray-tehr*

Idioms with être

Learning idiomatic expressions will enable you to sound more authentically French. Table 3.3 will show you some idioms with *être*.

Table 3.3   Idioms with être

French	Pronunciation	Meaning
être à	*ehtr ah*	to belong to
être d'accord (avec)	*ehtr dah-kohr*	to agree (with)
être en train de + infinitive	*ehtr ahN traN duh*	to be in the act of, busy
être sur le point de + infinitive	*ehtr sewr luh pwaN duh*	to be on the verge of

Attention!

Make sure to conjugate the verb when you use it in context:

Ce journal est à moi.   This newspaper is mine.

Je suis d'accord.   I agree.

Where Are You From?

Curiosity naturally prods us into asking other travelers for their place of origin, especially if we detect a foreign accent. Faraway lands always seem so exotic and exciting, and people love to talk about their hometowns. Use *être* to express where you are from. Use Tables 3.4 and 3.5 to find your place of origin.

Table 3.4 Feminine Countries

English	French	Pronunciation
Austria	l'Autriche	*lo-treesh*
China	la Chine	*lah sheen*
England	l'Angleterre	*lahN-gluh-tehr*
Germany	l'Allemagne	*lahl-mah-nyuh*
Greece	la Grèce	*lah grehs*
Italy	l'Italie	*lee-tah-lee*
Russia	la Russie	*lah rew-see*
Spain	l'Espagne	*lehs-pah-nyuh*

Full Speed Ahead

All feminine countries end in *-e*.

Table 3.5 Masculine Countries

English	French	Pronunciation
Canada	le Canada	*luh kah-nah-dah*
Israel	Israël	*eez-rah-ehl*

English	French	Pronunciation
Japan	le Japon	*luh zhah-pohN*
Mexico	le Mexique	*luh mehk-seek*
United States	les États-Unis	*lay zay-tah-zew-nee*

If your travels take you far and wide you are probably fortunate enough to be able to plan a trip to another continent. The names of the seven continents appear in Table 3.6.

Table 3.6   The Continents

English	French	Pronunciation
Africa	l'Afrique	*lah-freek*
Antarctica	l'Antarctique	*lahn-tahrk-teek*
Asia	l'Asie	*lah-zee*
Australia	l'Australie	*loh-strah-lee*
Europe	l'Europe	*lew-rohp*
North America	l'Amérique du Nord	*lah-may-reek dew nohr*
South America	l'Amérique du Sud	*lah-may-reek dew sewd*

Full Speed Ahead

L'Antarctique (Antarctica, *lahN-tahrk-teek*) is the only continent that is masculine.

Going to Stay?

The preposition *en* is used to express that you are going *to* or staying *in* another country. Use *en* to express *to*, and also to express *in* before the names of feminine countries, continents, provinces, islands, and states and before masculine countries starting with a vowel:

I am going to China.	I'm staying in Israel.
Je vais en Chine.	Je reste en Israël.

Use the preposition *au* (*aux* for plurals) to express *to, in* before the names of some masculine countries, islands, provinces, and states that start with a consonant:

I am going to Portugal.	I am staying in the United
Je vais au Portugal.	States.
	Je reste aux États-Unis.

Coming

If you want to say that you are from (or that you are coming from) a country, use the preposition *de* to express *from* before the names of feminine countries, continents, provinces, islands, and states and before masculine countries starting with a vowel:

I am from Belgium.	I am from Israel.
Je suis de Belgique.	Je suis d'Israël.

The preposition *de* + the definite article *(le, l', les)* is used to express *from* before masculine countries:

I am from Japan.	I am from the United States.
Je suis du Japon.	Je suis des États-Unis.

Near and Dear Ones

No introductory conversation is complete without a little bragging. How many times have you opened your wallet and started showing pictures of all your loved ones? It's almost second nature. Does it shock you to learn that many people actually enjoy seeing those corny pictures you carry with you? Use Table 3.7 to identify everyone correctly.

Table 3.7   Family Members

Male	French	Pronunciation
father	le père	*luh pehr*
grandfather	le grand-père	*luh grahN-pehr*
father-in-law	le beau-père	*luh bo-pehr*
child	l'enfant	*lahN-fahN*
brother	le frère	*luh frehr*
step-brother	le demi-frère	*luh duh-mee-frehr*
stepson, son-in-law	le beau-fils	*luh bo-fees*
son	le fils	*luh fees*
uncle	l'oncle	*lohNkl*
cousin	le cousin	*luh koo-zahN*
nephew	le neveu	*luh nuh-vuh*
husband	le mari	*luh mah-ree*
son-in-law	le gendre	*luh zhahNdr*
boyfriend	le petit ami	*luh puh-tee tah-mee*

Female	French	Pronunciation
mother	la mère	*lah mehr*
grandmother	la grand-mère	*lah graN-mehr*
mother-in-law	la belle-mère	*lah behl-mehr*
child	l'enfant	*lahN-fahN*
sister	la soeur	*lah suhr*
step-sister	la demi-soeur	*lah duh-mee-suhr*
step-daughter	la belle-fille	*lah behl-fee-y*
daughter	la fille	*lah fee-y*

continues

Table 3.7 Continued

Female	French	Pronunciation
aunt	la tante	*lah tahNt*
cousin	la cousine	*lah koo-zeen*
niece	la nièce	*lah nyehs*
wife	la femme	*lah fahm*
daughter-in-law	la belle-fille	*lah behl-fee-y*
girlfriend	la petite amie	*lah puh-tee tah-mee*

If the possessor is referred to not by name but by a common noun such as *the boy* or *the parents* (*He is the boy's father:* The father of the boy; or *That's the parents' car:* The car of the parents), then *de* contracts with the definite articles *le* and *les* to express *of the:*

| de + le | du | Ce sont le père *du* garçon. |
| de + les | des | C'est la voiture *des* parents. |

You Belong to Me

In English we use 's or s' to show possession after a noun. In French, however, there are no apostrophes. To translate "Marie's mother" into French, a speaker would have to say: "the mother of Marie," which is "la mère de Marie." The preposition *de* means *of* and is used to express possession or relationship.

Possessive Adjectives

The possessive adjectives *my*, *your*, *his*, *her*, and so on, can also be used to show possession as illustrated in Table 3.8:

Table 3.8 Possessive Adjectives

Used before masculine singular nouns or feminine singular nouns beginning with a vowel	Used before feminine singular nouns beginning with a consonant only	Used before all plural nouns
mon (*mohN*)/my	ma (*mah*)/my	mes (*may*)/my
ton (*tohN*)/your (fam.)	ta (*tah*)/your (fam.)	tes (*tay*)/your (fam.)
son (*sohN*)/his, her	sa (*sah*)/his, her	ses (*say*)/his, her
notre (*nohtr*)/our	notre (*nohtr*)/our	nos (*no*)/our
votre (*vohtr*)/your (pol.)	votre (*vohtr*)/your (pol.)	vos (*vo*)/your (pol.)
leur (*luhr*)/their	leur (*luhr*)/their	leurs (*luhr*)/their

Attention!

A possessive adjective must agree with the item possessed, not the possessor:

He loves *his* mother. Il aime *sa mère*.

She loves *her* mother. Elle aime *sa mère*.

He loves *his* father. Il aime *son père*.

She loves *her* father. Elle aime *son père*.

Son and *sa* both mean *his* or *her* because the possessive adjective agrees with the noun it modifies, not with the subject. Therefore, *her father* = *son père* because *son* agrees with the word *père*, which is masculine; and *his mother* = *sa mère* because *sa* agrees with the word *mère*, which is feminine.

What You Have

Perhaps you would like to discuss how many children you have or your age; or you might want to tell how you feel at a particular moment. The verb that you will find most helpful in these situations is *avoir* (to have). Like the verb *être* (to be), *avoir* is an irregular verb, and all of its forms (as seen in Table 3.9) must be memorized.

Table 3.9   The Verb avoir (to have)

French	Pronunciation	English
j'ai	*zhay*	I have
tu as	*tew ah*	you have
il, elle, on a	*eel,(ehl),(ohN) ah*	he, she, one has
nous avons	*noo zah-vohN*	we have
vous avez	*voo zah-vay*	you have
ils, elles ont	*eel, (ehlz) ohN*	they have

Idioms with avoir

The idiomatic expressions in Table 3.10 are used quite frequently in everyday conversation:

Table 3.10   Idioms with avoir

Idiom	Pronunciation	Meaning
avoir...ans	*ah-vwahr...ahN*	to be...years old
avoir besoin (de)	*ah-vwahr buh-zwaN duh*	to need
avoir chaud	*ah-vwahr sho*	to be hot (person)
avoir de la chance	*ah-vwahr duh lah shahNs*	to be lucky
avoir envie (de)	*ah-vwahr ahN-vee (duh)*	to need
avoir faim	*ah-vwahr faN*	to be hungry
avoir froid	*ah-vwahr frwah*	to be cold (person)

Idiom	Pronunciation	Meaning
avoir honte (de)	*ah-vwahr ohNt (duh)*	to be ashamed (of)
avoir l'air (+ adj.)	*ah-vwahr lehr*	to seem, look
avoir l'habitude de	*ah-vwahr lah-bee-tewd duh*	to be accustomed to
avoir l'intention de	*ah-vwahr laN-tahN-syohn duh*	to intend to
avoir l'occasion de	*ah-vwahr loh-kah-zyohN duh*	to have the opportunity to
avoir le temps de	*ah-vwahr luh tahN duh*	to have the time to
avoir lieu	*ah-vwahr lyuh*	to take place
avoir mal à	*ah-vwahr mahl ah*	to have an ache in
avoir peur (de)	*ah-vwahr puhr (duh)*	to be afraid (of)
avoir raison	*ah-vwahr reh-sohN*	to be right
avoir soif	*ah-vwahr swahf*	to be thirsty
avoir sommeil	*ah-vwahr soh-mehy*	to be sleepy
avoir tort	*ah-vwahr tohr*	to be wrong

Make sure to conjugate the verb when you use it in context:

J'ai l'occasion de voyager   I have the opportunity to travel.

Tu as de la chance.   You're lucky.

Asking Questions

If you don't want to seem too nosy and if your French is not as yet up to par, you'll probably be content to ask people simple yes or no questions. The four ways to do this are really quite easy.

An Extra Workout

I want to know all about you and my English is poor. Tell me as much as you can about yourself and your family in French. I'm very nosy, so don't leave out any details. Practice what you want to say until it flows smoothly.

Intonation

By far the easiest way to show that you're asking a question is to simply change your intonation by raising your voice at the end of the sentence.

Tu travailles aujourd'hui?   Are you working today?

N'est-ce pas?

Add the tag *n'est-ce pas* (*nehs pas*/isn't that so) at the end of the sentence:

Tu travailles aujourd'hui, n'est-ce pas?
You're working today, aren't you (isn't that so)?

Est-ce que

You may put *Est-ce que* (*ehs-kuh*) at the beginning of the sentence. Although it is not translated, *Est-ce que* does indicate that a question follows:

Est-ce que tu travailles aujourd'hui?

Inversion

Inversion, which is used far more frequently in writing than in conversation, means reversing the word order of the *subject pronoun* and the *conjugated verb form*. The rules governing inversion can get tricky—but don't despair. Use one of the other three methods mentioned if you want to make your life easy. You'll still be speaking perfectly correct French, you will be understood, and your question will be answered. If you are up to the challenge, here are the rules:

➤ **Avoid inverting with *je*.** It's awkward and is very rarely used.

➤ **You can ONLY invert subject pronouns with conjugated verbs. DO NOT invert with nouns!**

Tu travailles.	Travailles-tu?
Vous parlez français.	Parlez-vous français?
Elles habitent à Nice.	Habitent-elles à Nice?

➤ **With *il* and *elle* a -*t*- must be added to avoid having two vowels together.** This generally occurs only with verbs in the *er* family. The *il* and *elle* verb forms or *ir* and *re* verbs end in a consonant:

Il travaille bien.	Travaille-**t**-il bien?
Il choisit son dessert.	Choisit-il son dessert?
Elle rèpond vite.	Rèpond-elle vite?

Full Speed Ahead

Remember that whether you are using intonation, *est-ce que*, *n'est-ce pas*, or inversion, you are asking for exactly the same information: a yes/*oui* (*wee*) or no/*non* (*nohN*) answer:

Tu parles français?	Tu parles français, n'est-ce pas?
Est-ce que tu parles français?	Parles-tu français?

How to Answer

If the answer is yes, use *oui* (*wee*) and then give your statement:

Vous chantez?   Oui, je chante.

To answer yes to a negative quesion, use *si*.

Tu ne chantes pas bien?   Si, je chante bien.

If you want to say no, use *non* (*nohN*) and then add *ne* and *pas* (not), respectively, around the conjugated verb form. If there are two verbs, only the first is conjugated:

Vous dansez?   Non, je ne danse pas.
                              Non, je ne désire pas danser.

Put the following negative phrases around the conjugated verb if you want to vary your answers:

ne...jamais (*nuh...zhah-meh*)   never

Je ne fume jamais.   I never smoke.

ne...plus (*nuh...plew*)   no longer

Je ne fume plus.   I no longer smoke.
                                  (I don't smoke anymore.)

ne...rien (*nuh...ryaN*)   nothing, anything

Je ne fume rien.   I don't smoke anything.

Asking for Information

Are you curious, like me? Then a simple yes-no answer never suffices. You want to get the complete picture, and for that, you'll need the facts. Use the questions in Table 3.11 to get the scoop:

Table 3.11   Information Questions

French	Pronunciation	English
à quelle heure	*ah kehl uhr*	at what time
à qui	*ah kee*	to whom
à quoi	*ah kwah*	to what
avec qui	*ah-vehk kee*	with whom
avec quoi	*ah-vehk kwah*	with what
de qui	*duh kee*	of, about, from whom
de quoi	*duh kwah*	of, about, from what
combien (de + noun)	*kohN-byaN (duh)*	how much, many
comment	*kohN-mahN*	how
où	*oo*	where
d'où	*doo*	from where
pourquoi	*poor-kwah*	why
quand	*kahN*	when
qui	*kee*	who, whom
que	*kuh*	what
qu'est-ce que	*kehs-kuh*	what

Attention!

Use *que* at the beginning of a sentence and *quoi* at the end of a sentence to ask *what?*.

Qu'est-ce que tu fais?   Tu fais quoi?   What are you doing?

To ask for information:

➤ Use intonation.

Vous parlez (Tu parles) **avec qui**?

➤ Use *est-ce que.*

Avec qui est-ce que vous parlez (tu parles)?

➤ Use inversion.

Avec qui voyagez-vous (voyages-tu)?

An Extra Workout

It's your turn to be nosy. Write down a list of questions you would like to ask me. I'm a very interesting person, and I have a large family.

Chapter 4

At the Airport

In This Chapter

➤ On the airplane and in the airport

➤ All about *aller* (to go)

➤ Y

➤ Giving and receiving directions

➤ What to say when you don't understand

Be sure to comparison shop for your ticket when planning a trip by plane. An inexpensive non-refundable ticket isn't the bargain it's cracked up to be if you have to change your plans.

Plane rides can be long and tedious, especially when you cross time zones. All too often there are minor inconveniences and delays. The scenarios are endless. For any number of reasons you might prefer a different seat or have some typical tourist questions for the flight crew.

If you're lucky enough to be traveling on a foreign airline, you might want to use your knowledge of the language to help you get some tips and information. Use the terms in Table 4.1 to help you face any problem you might encounter:

Table 4.1   Inside the Plane

English	French	Pronunciation
aisle	le couloir	*luh kool-wahr*
(on the) aisle	côté couloir	*koh-tay kool-wahr*
to board, embark	embarquer	*ahN-bahr-kay*
crew	l'équipage (m.)	*lay-kee-pahzh*
to deplane	débarquer	*day-bahr-kay*
emergency exit	la sortie (l'issue) de secours	*lah sohr-tee (lee-sew) duh suh-koor*
gate	la porte	*lah pohrt*
landing	l'atterrissage	*lah-teh-ree-sahzh*
life vest	le gilet de sauvetage	*luh zhee-leh duh sohv-tahzh*
(non) smokers	(non) fumeurs	*(nohN) few-muhr*
row	le rang	*luh rahN*
seat	la place, le siège	*lah plahs, luh syehzh*
seatbelt	la ceinture de sécurité	*lah saN-tewr duh say-kew-ree-tay*
to smoke	fumer	*few-may*
takeoff	le décollage	*luh day-koh-lahzh*
(by the) window	côté fenêtre	*koh-tay fuh-nehtr*

After You've Landed

Expect to find plenty of signs pointing you in all the necessary directions. In anticipation of the rather lengthy time it takes to unload your baggage, where should you proceed first? How about the bathroom? Do you need some foreign currency? Are you famished after the delicious culinary repast you received in flight? Table 4.2 provides all the words you need to know once you are inside the airport.

Table 4.2   Inside the Airport

English	French	Pronunciation
airline	la ligne aérienne	*lah lee-nyuh ahy-ryehn*
airline terminal	l'aérogare (f.), le terminal	*lahy-roh-gahr, luh tehr-mee-nahl*
airplane	l'avion (m.)	*lah-vyohN*
airport	l'aéroport	*luhy-roh-pohr*
arrival	l'arrivée	*lah-ree-vay*
baggage claim area	la bande, les bagages (m.)	*lah bahnde, lay bah-gahzh*
bathrooms	les toilettes (f.)	*lay twah-leht*
bus stop	l'arrêt de bus	*lah-reh duh bews*
car rental	la location de voitures	*lah loh-kah-syohN duh vwah-tewr*
carry-on luggage	les bagages à main	*lay-bah-gahzh ah maN*
cart	le chariot	*luh shah-ryoh*
counter	le comptoir	*luh kohN-twahr*
departure	le départ	*luh day-pahr*
destination	la destination	*lah dehs-tee-nah-syohN*
elevators	les ascenseurs (m.)	*lay-zah-sahN-suhr*
entrance	l'entrée	*lahN-tray*
exit	la sortie	*lah-sohr-tee*
flight	le vol	*luh vohl*
gate	la porte	*lah pohrt*

continues

Table 4.2 Continued

English	French	Pronunciation
information	les renseignements (m.)	*lay rahN-seh-nyuh-mahN*
lost and found	les objets trouvés	*lay zohb-zheh troo-vay*
to miss the flight	manquer (rater) le vol	*mahN-kay (rah-tay) luh vohl*
money exchange	le bureau de change	*luh bew-ro duh shahNzh*
passport control	le contrôle des passeports	*luh kohN-trohl day pahs-pohr*
porter	le porteur	*luh pohr-tuhr*
security check	le contrôle de sécurité	*luh kohN-trohl duh say-kew-ree-tay*
stop-over	l'escale	*lehs-kahl*
suitcase	la valise	*lah vah-leez*
taxis	les taxis	*lay tahk-see*
ticket	le billet, le ticket	*luh bee-yeh, luh tee-keh*
trip	le voyage	*luh vwah-yahzh*

Where Are You Going?

Getting lost in today's modern, sprawling international airports is rather easy. To find your way around, you'll need to know how to ask the right questions.

Où est le comptoir?
oo eh luh kohN-twahr?
Where is the counter?

Le comptoir, s'il vous plaît.
luh kohN-twahr seel voo pleh.
The counter, please.

Où sont les bagages?
oo sohN lay bah-gahzh?
Where is the baggage claim?

Les bagages, s'il vous plaît.
lay bah-gahzh seel voo pleh.
The baggage claim, please.

If the place you are trying to find is near you, expect to hear:

Voici le comptoir.   Voilà le comptoir.
vwah-see luh kohN-twahr.   *vwah-lah luh kohN-twahr.*
Here is the counter.   There is the counter.

One verb that will really come in handy is shown in Table 4.3. *Aller* (to go), is an irregular verb that must be memorized.

Table 4.3   The Verb aller (to go)

French	Pronunciation	English
je vais	*zhuh veh*	I go
tu vas	*tew vah*	you go
il, elle, on va	*eel, (ehl) (ohN) vah*	he, she, one goes
nous allons	*noo zah-lohN*	we go
vous allez	*voo zah-lay*	you go
ils, elles vont	*eel (ehl) vohN*	they go

Y

Y, a pronoun meaning *there*, generally replaces the preposition *à (au, a l', à la, aux)* or other prepositions of location: *chez*-at the house (business) of, *contre*-against, *dans*-in, *derrière*-behind, *devant*-in front of, *en*-in, *entre*-between, *sous*-under, *sur*-on, *vers*-toward. *Y* can also mean it, them, in it/them, to it/them, or on it/them.

Tu vas à Rome.   Mon stylo est sur la table.   Je réponds au téléphone.

Tu *y* vas.   Mon stylo *y* est.   J'*y* réponds.
You go there.   My pen is on it (there).   I answer it.

Attention!

Never use *y* to refer to people. *Y* only refers to places, things, or ideas.

Complications

When where you want to get to is not within pointing distance, you'll need further directions. The verbs in Table 4.4 can help you get where you want to go or can help you aide someone else who is lost.

Table 4.4 Verbs Giving Directions

French	Pronunciation	English
aller	*ah-lay*	to go
continuer	*kohN-tee-new-ay*	to continue
descendre	*day-sahNdr*	to go down
marcher	*mahr-shay*	to walk
monter	*mohN-tay*	to go up
passer	*pah-say*	to pass
prendre	*prahNdr*	to take
tourner	*toor-nay*	to turn
traverser	*trah-vehr-say*	to cross

Use either *tu* (singular) or *vous* (plural) as the subject of your command. Since the subject of a command is always understood to be *you*, drop the tu or vous and use the correct verb form. For *er* verbs only, drop the final *s* from the *tu* form in all commands.

Tourne à gauche.	Allez tout droit.
Turn to the left.	Go straight ahead.

Excuse Me. What Did You Say?

Suppose someone gives you directions, and you just don't
understand? The person with whom you are speaking
could be mumbling, speaking at a rapid-fire pace, have a
strong regional accent, or use unfamiliar words. There's
no cause for embarrassment. The phrases in Table 4.5
can be an invaluable aid if you need to have something
repeated or if you need more information.

Table 4.5   When You Don't Understand

French	Pronunciation	English
Excusez (Excuse)-moi	*ehk-skew-zay (ehk-skewz) mwah*	Excuse me
Pardon	*pahr-dohN*	Pardon me
Je ne comprends pas	*zhuh nuh kohN-prahN pah*	I don't understand
Je ne vous (t') ai pas entendu.	*zhuh nuh voo zay (tay) pah zahN-tahN-dew*	I didn't hear you
Répétez (Répète), s'il vous (te) plaît	*ray-pay-tay (ray-peht) seel voo (tuh) pleh*	Please repeat it
Parlez (Parle) plus lentement.	*pahr-lay (pahrl) plew lahNt-mahN*	Speak more slowly
Qu'est-ce que vous avez (tu as) dit?	*kehs-kuh voo zah-vay (tew ah) dee?*	What did you say?

An Extra Workout

Study your phrases and then close this book (but keep your finger on the page). Pretend someone is speaking to you very quickly and you just don't understand. Use as many phrases as you can remember to express your lack of comprehension. You can peek, if you must.

Chapter 5

Getting Wherever You're Going

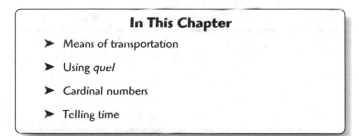

In This Chapter

➤ Means of transportation

➤ Using *quel*

➤ Cardinal numbers

➤ Telling time

If you're traveling in a French-speaking country, you can take advantage of several different means of transportation to get to your destination. Ask yourself the following questions: Are you traveling light? In that case, you might want to mingle with people and take buses, subways, and trains. How tight is your budget and how much time do you have? If money is no object or if you're in a hurry, a taxi might be your best option. Do you enjoy seeing the countryside? If you're confident and are familiar with foreign traffic laws and street signs, you might just want to rent a car.

To say how you're getting there use the irregular verb *prendre* (see Table 5.1). *Prendre* has a tricky pronunciation: All singular forms end in a nasal sound, but the third person plural, *ils/elles*, is pronounced quite differently. The double *n*s eliminate the need for an initial nasal sound and give the first *e* a more open sound.

Table 5.1   The Verb prendre (to take)

English	French	Pronunciation
I take	je prends	*zhuh prahN*
you take	tu prends	*tew prahN*
he, she, one takes	il, elle, on prend	*eel (ehl) (ohN) prahN*
we take	nous prenons	*noo pruh-nohN*
you take	vous prenez	*voo pruh-nay*
they take	ils, elles prennent	*eel (ehl) prehn*

Now you're ready to say how you're getting there:

> I take...
> Je prends...
> *zhuh phraN*

English	French	Pronunciation
the boat	le bateau	*luh bah-to*
the bus	le bus (l'autobus)	*le bews (loh-to-bews)*
the car	l'auto (f.)	*lo-to*
the car	la voiture	*lah vwah-tewr*
the subway	le métro	*luh may-tro*
taxi	le taxi	*le tahk-see*
train	le train	*luh traN*

If You're Traveling by Bus:

If its Paris you're visiting, the R.A.T.P. (Régie Autonome des Transports Parisiens) directs the user-friendly bus and subway system. Green Parisian buses post their route and destination on the outside, front of the bus and their major stops on the bus's sides. The route of each line is indicated on a sign at every stop it makes. Free bus maps (autobus Paris—Plan du Réseau) are readily available at tourist offices and some métro booths. Since tickets may not be purchased aboard the bus, they must be bought ahead of time at a métro station or bureau de tabac (tobacconist).

Where is the nearest bus stop?
Où est l'arrêt de bus le plus proche?
oo eh lah-reh duh bews luh plew prohsh

How much is the fare?
Combien coûte un billet?
kohN-byaN koo tuhN bee-yeh

If You're Traveling by Subway:

Even more efficient are the 13 numbered subway lines, indicated by different colors on subway maps distributed everywhere: at métro stops, hotels, department stores, tourist offices. Each métro station displays a **plan du quartier**, a detailed map of the surrounding area. Transfers from one subway line to another are free, and connections are indicated by orange **correspondance** signs. You may transfer as often as you like on one ticket, provided that you do not exit to the street. Exits are clearly marked by blue **sortie** signs.

Where is the nearest subway?
Où se trouve la station de métro la plus proche?
oo suh troov lah stah-syohN duh may-tro lah plew prohsh

Where can I buy a ticket?
Où puis-je acheter un billet?
oo pweezh ahsh-tay uhN bee-yeh

How much is the fare?
Quel est le prix du trajet?
kehl eh luh pree dew trah-zheh

How many more stops are there?
Il reste combien d'arrêts?
eel rehst kohN-byaN dah-reh

What's the next station?
Quelle est la prochaine station?
kehl eh lah proh-sehn stah-syohN

Where can I find a subway map?
Où puis-je trouver un plan du métro?
oo pweezh troo-vay uhN plahN dew may-tro

If You're Traveling by Taxi:

Taxis always gives a flat rate from the airport (for other trips, it's metered) but charge extra for handling luggage and may refuse to accept more than three passengers.

Where is the nearest taxi stand?
Où est l'arrêt de taxi le plus proche?
oo eh lah-reh duh tahk-see luh plew prohsh

Would you please call me a cab?
Appelez-moi un taxi s'il vous plaît.
ah-play mwah uhN tahk-see seel voo pleh

I would like to go...	How much is it to...
Je voudrais aller...	C'est combien pour aller à...
zhuh voo-dreh zah-lay	*seh kohN-byaN poor ah-lay ah*
Stop here.	Wait for me.
Arrêtez-vous ici.	Espérez-moi.
ah-reh-tay voo zee-see	*ehs-pay-ray mwah*

If You're Traveling by Train:

If you're going farther afield, the R.A.T.P. also provides service on the R.E.R (Réseau Express Régional), the local suburban train system. The S.N.C.F. (Société Nationale des Chemins de Fer) boasts trains that are the fastest in the world. The popular T.G.V. (train à grande vitesse), travels within the entire country, and links Paris to the rest of the cities in France. It has attained the world record of 260 kilometers (162 miles) an hour.

Where is the nearest train station?
Où est la gare la plus proche?
oo eh lah gahr lah plew prohsh

I would like...
Je voudrais...
zhuh voo-dreh...

a first (second) class ticket.
un billet de première (deuxième) classe
uhN bee-yeh duh pruh-myehr (duhz-yehm) klahs

a round-trip ticket.
un aller-retour
uhN nah-lay ruh-toor

a (non) smoking compartment
un compartiment (non) fumeurs
uhN kohN-pahr-tce-mahN (nohN) few-muhr

Is it a local (express)?
Est-ce un local (un express)?
ehs uhN loh-kahl (uhN nehks-prehs)

From what platform does it leave?
De quel quai part-il?
duh kehl keh pahr-teel

If You're Traveling by Car:

Driving in Paris can be treacherous: The drivers are unpredictable, the traffic is congested and there are **very** few parking spots. If you're daring, go to *une location de voitures* to rent a car. Always compare before you make a final choice. Don't be surprised when the price at the gas pump is almost double what you generally pay back home.

I would like to rent a…
Je voudrais louer une (give make of car).
zhuh voo-dreh loo-ay ewn

I prefer automatic transmission.
Je préfère la transmission automatique.
zhuh pray-fehr lah tranhz-mee-syohN o-toh-mah-teek.

How much does it cost per day (per week) (per kilometer)?
Quel est le tarif à la journée (à la semaine) (au kilomètre)?
kehl eh luh tah-reef ah lah zhoor-nay (ah la suh-mehn) (o kee-lo-mehtr)

How much is the insurance?
Quel est le montant de l'assurance?
kehl eh luh mohn-tahN duh lah-sew-rahNs

Is the gas included?
Le carburant est compris?
luh kahr-bew-rahN eh kohN-pree

Do you accept credit cards? Which ones?
Acceptez-vous des cartes de crédit? Lesquelles?
ahk-sehp-tay voo day kahrt duh kray-dee/lay-kehl

Do you fill it up with gas?
Vous faites le plein d'essence?
voo feht luh plaN deh-sahNs

Attention!

Take a piece of advice from me if you've decided to rent a
car. Inspect the entire car very carefully—both inside and
out. Once you're on the road, there's no telling what
could go wrong. Open the trunk and make sure there's a
jack—*un cric* (*uhN kreek*) and a spare tire—*un pneu de
secours* (*uhN pnuh duh suh-koor*).

Kilometers measure distance in Europe. Refer to Table 5.2
for the approximate equivalents.

Table 5.2 Distance Measures (Approximate)

Miles	Kilometers	Miles	Kilometers
.62	1	12	20
3	5	31	50
6	10	62	100

The French word *feu* refers to a traffic light. Stop *au feu
rouge* (at the red light) and go *au feu vert* (at the green
light). Should a *gendarme* stop you for a traffic infraction
try using your foreign nationality as an excuse: *Mais, je
suis américain(e)*. Sometimes a simple apology can work:
Pardon (Excusez-moi). Je le regrette.

Heading in the Right Direction

Learn those road signs—some are not as obvious as you'd
think. Familiarize yourself with the following before you
venture out on your own:

You also need to know your compass directions:

to the north	to the east	to the south	to the west
au nord	à l'est	au sud	à l'ouest
o nohr	*ah lehst*	*o sewd*	*ah lwehst*

Full Speed Ahead

To ask questions about the mode of transportation you've chosen, you'll use the interrogative adjective *quel* (which, what), which like other adjectives, agrees with the noun it modifies.

	Masculine	Feminine
Singular	quel	quelle
Plural	quels	quelles

How Much Is It?

You'll need to learn the French numbers listed in Table 5.3 to express which flight or bus you are taking or to figure out how much a rental car is going to cost you. You'll need these very same numbers when you want to tell time, count to ten, or reveal your age.

Table 5.3   Cardinal Numbers

French	Pronunciation	English
zéro	*zay-ro*	0
un	*uhN*	1
deux	*duh*	2
trois	*trwah*	3
quatre	*kahtr*	4
cinq	*saNk*	5
six	*sees*	6

continues

Table 5.3 Continued

French	Pronunciation	English
sept	*seht*	7
huit	*weet*	8
neuf	*nuhf*	9
dix	*dees*	10
onze	*ohNz*	11
douze	*dooz*	12
treize	*trehz*	13
quatorze	*kah-tohrz*	14
quinze	*kaNz*	15
seize	*sehz*	16
dix-sept	*dee-seht*	17
dix-huit	*dee-zweet*	18
dix-neuf	*dee-znuhf*	19
vingt	*vaN*	20
vingt et un	*vaN tay uhN*	21
vingt-deux	*vaN-duh*	22
trente	*trahNt*	30
quarante	*kah-rahNt*	40
cinquante	*saN-kahNt*	50
soixante	*swah-sahNt*	60
soixante-dix	*swah-sahNt-dees*	70
soixante et onze	*swah-sahNt ay ohNz*	71
soixante-douze	*swah-sahNt-dooz*	72
soixante-treize	*swah-sahNt-trehz*	73
soixante-quatorze	*swah-sahNt-kah-tohrz*	74
soixante-quinze	*swah-sahNt-kaNz*	75
soixante-seize	*swah-sahNt-sehz*	76
soixante-dix-sept	*swah-sahNt-dee-seht*	77

French	Pronunciation	English
soixante-dix-huit	*swah-sahNt-dee-zweet*	78
soixante-dix-neuf	*swah-sahNt-dee-znuf*	79
quatre-vingts	*kahtr-vaN*	80
quatre-vingt-un	*kahtr-vaN-uhN*	81
quatre-vingt-deux	*kahtr-vaN-duh*	82
quatre-vingt-dix	*kahtr-vaN-dees*	90
quatre-vingt-onze	*kahtr-vaN-onze*	91
quatre-vingt-douze	*kahtr-vaN-dooz*	92
cent	*sahN*	100
cent un	*sahN uhN*	101
deux cents	duh sahN	200
deux cent un	*duh sahN uhN*	201
mille	*meel*	1000
deux mille	*duh meel*	2000
un million	*uhN meel-yohN*	1,000,000
deux millions	*duh meel-yohN*	2,000,000
un milliard	*uhN meel-yahr*	1,000,000,000
deux milliards	*duh meel-yahr*	2,000,000,000

Attention!

The French write the number 1 with a little hook on top. To distinguish a 1 from a 7, they put a line through the 7 when they write it: 7.

In numerals and decimals, where we use commas the French use periods and vice versa:

English	French
1,000	1.000
.25	0,25
$9.95	$9,95

French numbers are somewhat tricky until you get used to them. Look carefully at Table 5.5 and pay special attention to the following:

➤ The conjunction *et* (and) is used only for the numbers 21, 31, 41, 51, 61, and 71. Use a hyphen in all other compound numbers through 99.

➤ *Un* becomes *une* before a feminine noun:

   vingt et un garçons et vingt et une filles

➤ To form 71-79, use 60 + 11, 12, 13, and so on.

➤ To form 91-99, use 80 (4 20s) + 11, 12, 13, and so on.

➤ Do not use *un* (one) before *cent* and *mille*.

➤ *Mille* doesn't change in the plural.

Do You Have the Time?

Now that you have the hang of French numbers, it should be rather easy to express the time, as explained below in Table 5.4.

What time is it?	At what time?
Quelle heure est-il?	À quelle heure?
kehl uhr eh-teel?	*ah kehl uhr*

Table 5.4   Telling Time

French	Pronunciation	English
Il est une heure.	*eel eh tewn nuhr*	It is 1:00.
Il est deux heures cinq.	*eel eh duh zuhr saNk*	It is 2:05.
Il est trois heures dix.	*eel eh trwah zuhr dees*	It is 3:10.
Il est quatre heures et quart.	*eel eh kahtr uhr ay kahr*	It is 4:15.
Il est cinq heures vingt.	*eel eh saN kuhr vaN*	It is 5:20.
Il est six heures vingt-cinq	*eel eh see zuhr vaN-suNk*	It is 6:25.
Il est sept heures et demie.	*eel eh seh tuhr ay duh-mee*	It is 7:30.
Il est huit heures moins vingt-cinq.	*eel eh wee tuhr mwaN vaN-saNk*	It is 7:35.
Il est neuf heures moins vingt.	*eel eh nuh vuhr mwaN vaN*	It is 8:40.
Il est dix heures moins le quart.	*eel eh dee zuhr mwaN luh kahr*	It is 9:45.
Il est onze heures moins dix.	*eel eh ohN zuhr mwaN dees*	It is 10:50.
Il est midi moins cinq.	*eel eh mee-dee mwaN saNk*	It is 11:55.
Il est minuit.	*eel eh mee-nwee*	It is midnight.

When telling time be sure to do the following:

➤ Simply add the number of minutes to express the time after the hour; use *et* only with *quart* et *demi(e)*.

➤ Use *moins le* (before, less, minus) to express time before the hour.

➤ Use the following to express half past noon or midnight:

Il est midi et demi.

Il est minuit et demi.

➤ *Demie* is used to express half past with all other hours.

An Extra Workout

Look in your local newspaper and, in French, read aloud the movie times for the films you want to see.

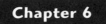

Chapter 6

Hotel Happiness

In This Chapter

➤ Getting the most from your hotel

➤ Ordinal numbers

A U.S. travel agent can help you find accommodations and make reservations that suit both your needs and your budget, no matter where you go in the French-speaking world. Should you have a spur of the moment change of plans, you can always go to a Syndicat d'initiative (*saN-dee-kah dee-nee-see-yah-tive*) or an Office du Tourisme to procure a room. You can expect to find the following types of lodgings in your travels:

➤ *Hotels* are rated by The French National Tourist Office, which provides an official government guide granting ratings from 1 star (very modest) to 4 stars (deluxe). The accommodations and amenities the hotel offers, as well as its location determine the number of stars it receives.

➤ *Motels* are becoming increasingly popular in France. Expect to find them at the airport and near main roads in rural areas and outside large cities.

➤ *Pensions* are cozy, comfortable establishments that are usually family-run businesses. They provide anything from the bare minimum in services to the very luxurious. Their prices may include food and lodging. Staying in a pension is for the traveler who really wants to get to know the country by taking the path that's less traveled.

➤ *Auberges* are popular roadside inns, which generally provide services for people traveling by car. An *auberge de jeunesse* is a youth hostel which provides a dormitory setting.

➤ *Chambres d'hôte* are "bed-and-breakfasts" (usually in the proprietor's house) that are maintained by local families in small towns and villages.

➤ *Gîtes Ruraux* are private homes or apartments that are for rent.

It's always a good idea to check with your travel agency or the hotel's management before leaving home, to make sure all the amenities you require are available. Depending upon your needs, you'll want to know the words for everything from bathroom to swimming pool. Be prepared for some surprises, even with reservations and assurances from your agent. Remember that it never hurts to ask questions when you are making arrangements or when you are in doubt. See Table 6.1 for a basic list of hotel amenities:

Table 6.1   Hotel Facilities

English	French	Pronunciation
bar	le bar	*luh bahr*
bellman	le bagagiste	*luh bah-gahzh-eest*
business center	le centre d'affaires	*luh sahNtr dah-fehr*
cashier	la caisse	*lah kehs*
concierge (caretaker)	le (la) concierge	*luh (lah) kohN-syehrzh*
doorman	le portier	*luh pohr-tyay*
elevator	l'ascenseur (m.)	*lah-sahN-suhr*
fitness center	le club santé	*luh klewb sahN-tay*
gift shop	la boutique	*lah boo-teek*
maid service	la gouvernante	*lah goo-vehr-nahNt*
restaurant	le restaurant	*luh rehs-toh-rahN*
staircase	l'escalier (m.)	*lehs-kahl-yay*
swimming pool	la piscine	*lah pee-seen*
valet parking	l'attendance (f.) du garage	*lah-tahN-dahNs dew gah-rahzh*

Attention!

In French buildings the ground floor is called **le rez-de-chausée** (abbreviated rez-de-ch) and the basement is called **le sous-sol** (abbreviated s-s). The "first floor" is really on the second story of any building.

Getting What You Want

Is something missing? Are you dissatisfied with your accommodations? If you need something to make your stay more enjoyable, don't be afraid to speak up. Table 6.2 lists a few items you might want or need:

I would like...	Je voudrais...	*zhuh voo-dreh*
I need...	Il me faut...	*eel muh foh*
I need...	J'ai besoin de (d')	*zhay buh zwaN duh*
Please send me...	Veuillez m'envoyer...	*vuh-yay mahN-vwah-yay*
There isn't (aren't)...	Il n'y a pas de...	*eel nyah pah duh*

Don't forget to show good manners by using the following phrases:

please	thank you	
s'il vous plaît	merci beaucoup	
seel voo pleh	*mehr-see bo-koo*	

you're welcome	you're welcome	don't mention it
de rien	pas de quoi	Je vous en prie.
duh ryaN	*pahd kwah*	*zhuh voo zahN pree*

Table 6.2   Wants and Needs

English	French	Pronunciation
air conditioning	la climatisation	*lah klee-mah-tee-zah-syohN*
an ashtray	un cendrier	*uhN sahN-dree-yay*
a balcony	un balcon	*uhN bahl-kohN*
a bar of soap	une savonnette	*ewn sah-voh-neht*
a bathroom	une salle de bains	*ewn sahl duh baN*
a blanket	une couverture	*ewn koo-vehr-tewr*

English	French	Pronunciation
hangers	des cintres	*deh saNtr*
a key	une clé (clef)	*ewn klay (klay)*
ice cubes	des glaçons	*deh glah-sohn*
on the courtyard	côté cour	*koh-tay koor*
on the garden	côté jardin	*koh-tay zhahr-daN*
on the sea	côté mer	*koh-tay mehr*
a pillow	un oreiller	*uhN noh-reh-yay*
a safe (deposit box)	un coffre	*uhN kohfr*
a shower	une douche	*ewn doosh*
a single (double) room	une chambre à un (deux) lits	*ewn shahNbr ah uhN (duh) lee*
a telephone	un téléphone	*uhN tay-lay-fohn*
a television (color)	une télévision (en couleurs)	*ewn tay-lay-vee-zyohN (ahN koo-luhr)*
tissues	des mouchoirs en papier	*day moo-shwahr ahN pah-pyay*
toilet paper	un rouleau de papier hygiénique	*uhN roo-lo duh pah-pyay ee-zhyay-neek*
a towel	une serviette	*ewn sehr-vyeht*
a beach towel	un drap de bain	*uhN drah duh baN*
a transformer	un transformateur	*uhN trahnz-fohr-mah-tuhr*

An Extra Workout

After studying Table 6.2, pretend you are in a hotel and need or want something. You find it necessary to call the front desk. Try to recall as many vocabulary words as possible so you can ask for these things.

Up, Up, and Away

I'd bet that like most of us, you've had an elevator experience, either in a hotel or elsewhere—in which you've felt like a large sardine in a small can. When you're pushed to the back or squished to the side, you have to hope that a kind and gentle soul will wiggle a hand free and ask: *Quel étage, s'il vous plaît (kehl ay-tahzh seel voo pleh)*? You will need the ordinal numbers in Table 6.3 to give a correct answer, such as: *Le troisième étage, s'il vous plaît (luh trwah-zyehm ay-tahzh see voo pleh)*.

Table 6.3   Ordinal Numbers

French	Pronunciation	English
premier (première)	*pruh-myay (pruh-myehr)*	1st
deuxième (second[e])	*duh-zyehm (suh-gohN[d])*	2nd
troisième	*trwah-zyehm*	3rd
quatrième	*kah-tree-yehm*	4th
cinquième	*saN-kyehm*	5th
sixième	*see-zyehm*	6th
septième	*seh-tyehm*	7th
huitième	*wee-tyehm*	8th
neuvième	*nuh-vyehm*	9th
dixième	*dee-zyehm*	10th
onzième	*ohN-zyehm*	11th
douzième	*doo-zyehm*	12th
vingtième	*vaN-tyehm*	20th
vingt et un(e)ième	*vaN-tay-uhN (ewn)-nyehm*	21st
soixante-douzième	*swah-sahNt doo-zyehm*	72nd
centième	*sahN-tyehm*	100th

➤ The only ordinal numbers that must agree in gender (masculine or feminine) with the noun they describe are *premier* and *second*.

son premier roman	his (her) first novel
sa première chanson	his (her) first song

➤ Except for *premier* and *second*, add *ième* to all cardinal numbers to form the ordinal number. Drop the silent *e* before *ième*.

➤ Observe that *u* was added in *cinquième*, and *v* replaced *f* in *neuvième*.

➤ *Second(e)* is generally used in a series that does not go beyond two.

➤ Elision (the definite article *le* or *la* does not drop its vowel) does not occur with *huitième* and *onzième*.

le huitième mois	the eighth month
la onzième année	the eleventh year

An Extra Workout

Open a book you have handy. Look at the page number and state it in French. Repeat this two times.

Chapter 7

What a Gorgeous Day!

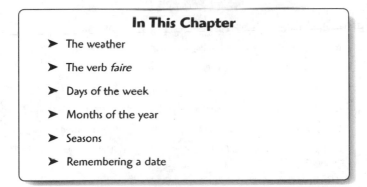

In This Chapter

➤ The weather

➤ The verb *faire*

➤ Days of the week

➤ Months of the year

➤ Seasons

➤ Remembering a date

Trips are taken all over the world year-round. No matter when that special time may fall, you should familiarize yourself with the weather conditions to expect, so that you can plan and pack properly. And after you arrive in a country, you'll want to be able to read or listen to the weather forecast (la météo—*lah may-tay-o*) so you can arrange your sightseeing trips and outings accordingly. The phrases in Table 7.1 will help you with the weather.

Table 7.1 Weather Expressions

French	Pronunciation	English
Quel temps fait-il?	*kehl tahN feh-teel*	What's the weather?
Il fait beau.	*eel feh bo*	It's beautiful.
Il fait chaud.	*eel feh sho*	It's hot.
Il fait du soleil.	*eel feh dew soh-lehy*	It's sunny.
Il fait mauvais.	*eel feh moh-veh*	It's nasty (bad).
Il fait froid.	*eel feh frwah*	It's cold.
Il fait frais.	*eel feh freh*	It's cool.
Il fait du vent.	*eel feh dew vahN*	It's windy.
Il fait des éclairs (m.)	*eel feh day zay-klehr*	It's lightning.
Il fait du tonnerre.	*eel feh dew toh-nehr*	It's thundering.
Il y a du brouillard.	*eel yah dew broo-yahr*	It's foggy.
Il fait humide.	*eel feh tew-meed*	It's humid.
Il y a des nuages.	*eel yah day new-ahzh*	It's cloudy.
Le ciel est couvert.	*luh syehl eh koo-vehr*	It's overcast.
Il pleut.	*eel pluh*	It's raining.
Il pleut à verse.	*eel pluh ah vehrs*	It's pouring.
Il neige.	*eel nehzh*	It's snowing.
Il y a des rafales (f.)	*eel yah day rah-fahl*	There are gusts of wind.
Il y a de la grêle.	*eel yah duh lah grehl*	There's hail.
Il y a des giboulées (f.)	*eel yah day zhee-boo-lay*	There are sudden showers.

Just How Hot or Cold Is It?

You might get confused when you hear the temperature in a French-speaking country. That's because they use the Celsius scale rather than the Fahrenheit scale to which we are accustomed. This means that when the concierge tells you it's 20 degrees (Celsius), it's really a balmy 68 degrees Fahrenheit. To ask for the temperature simply say:

Il fait quelle temperature?
eel feh kehl tahN-pay-rah-tewr
What's the temperature?

Rather than walk around with a mini-calculator, why not refer to the following thermometer for a general idea of what the weather is like:

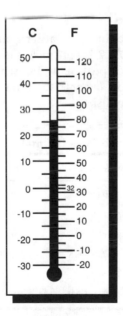

Now here are possible answers to your question:

Il fait moins dix.	Il fait zéro.	Il fait soixante.
eel feh mwaN dees	*eel feh zay-ro*	*eel feh swah-sahNt*
It's 10 below.	It's zero.	It's sixty degrees.

An Extra Workout

Look at the weather map in your daily newspaper. Give the weather and temperature in French for cities throughout the country.

The Verb Faire

When you speak about the weather, you need the verb *faire*. Shown in Table 7.2, *faire* means *to make* or *to do*, and is also often used to speak about household chores and about playing a sport (even though in this case it translates poorly into English).

Table 7.2   The Verb faire (to make, to do)

French	Pronunciation	English
je fais	*zhuh feh*	I make, do
tu fais	*tew feh*	you make, do
il, elle, on fait	*eel (ehl, ohN) feh*	he (she, one) makes, does
nous faisons	*noo fuh-zohN*	we make, do
vous faites	*voo feht*	you make, do
ils, elles font	*eel (ehl) fohN*	they make, do

Expressions with faire

A major goal of yours is to speak French idiomatically, the way natives do. Table 7.3 will give you some very handy idiomatic expressions with *faire:*

Table 7.3   More Idioms with faire

French	Pronunciation	English
faire attention à	*fehr ah-tahN-syohN ah*	to pay attention to
faire des achats (emplettes)	*fehr day zah-shah (ahN-pleht)*	to go shopping
faire la connaissance de	*fehn lah koh-neh-sahNs duh*	to meet, become acquainted with
faire la queue	*fehr lah kuh*	to stand in line
faire une partie de	*fehr ewn pahr-tee duh*	to play a game of
faire une promenade	*fehr ewn prohm-nahd*	to take a walk
faire un voyage	*fehr uhN vwah-yahzh*	to take a trip

You must conjugate *faire* when you use it in context:

Tu fais un voyage?   Are you taking a trip?

Elles font une promenade.   They are taking a walk.

What Day Is It?

You're definitely more likely to forget the day of the week when you are very preoccupied or busy. It's extremely important to keep track of the day when you're traveling so you don't wind up at a tourist attraction you absolutely had to see on the day it's closed. Study the days of the week in Table 7.4 so you don't miss out on anything.

In French, only capitalize days of the week when they are at the beginning of a sentence. When used elsewhere, unlike in English, they are written with a lower-case first letter.

Samedi est un jour.   Je vais au supermarché le
Saturday is a day.   samedi.
                         I go to the supermarket on
                         Saturday.

To express *on* when talking about a certain day, the French use the indefinite article *le:*

> Le mardi il va au centre commercial.
> *luh mahr-dee eel veh o sahNtr koh-mehr-syahl*
> On Tuesday(s) he goes to the mall.

Table 7.4   Days of the Week

English	French	Pronunciation
Monday	lundi	*luhN-dee*
Tuesday	mardi	*mahr-dee*
Wednesday	mercredi	*mehr-kruh-dee*
Thursday	jeudi	*zhuh-dee*
Friday	vendredi	*vahN-druh-dee*
Saturday	samedi	*sahm-dee*
Sunday	dimanche	*dee-mahNsh*

Unlike our calendars, French calendars start with Monday. Don't let this confuse you when you give a quick glance. You want to make sure that you get to that appointment on the right day.

My Favorite Month

As you eagerly peruse glossy vacation brochures, you'll probably be wondering about the best time to take your trip. Table 7.5 gives you the names of the months so you don't wind up in the wrong place at the wrong time.

Table 7.5   Months of the Year

English	French	Pronunciation
January	janvier	*zhahN-vyay*
February	février	*fay-vree-yay*

English	French	Pronunciation
March	mars	*mahrs*
April	avril	*ah-vreel*
May	mai	*meh*
June	juin	*zhwaN*
July	juillet	*zhwee-eh*
August	août	*oo(t)*
September	septembre	*schp-tahNbr*
October	octobre	*ohk-tohbr*
November	novembre	*noh-vahNbr*
December	décembre	*day-sahNbr*

Unless used at the beginning of a sentence, the names of all months should be written in lower-case.

Janvier est un mois.   Je vais en France en janvier.
January is a month.   I go to France in January.

To make it clear that something is expected to happen *in* a certain month, use the preposition *en*.

We are going to Europe in September.
Nous allons en Europe en septembre.

To Every Season Turn, Turn, Turn

Weather-wise, some seasons are better than others for traveling in certain countries. Make sure to plan your trip for when the weather will be great, so you don't have to worry about hurricanes, storms, or other adverse conditions. Table 7.6 provides the names of the seasons.

Table 7.6   The Seasons

English	French	Pronunciation
winter	l'hiver	*lee-vehr*
spring	le printemps	*luh praN-tahN*
summer	l'été	*lay-tay*
autumn, fall	l'automne	*lo-tohn*

The French use the preposition *en* for all the seasons to express *in*, except for spring, when *au* is used:

Elle va à Paris en hiver (en été, en automne, **au** printemps).
She's going to Paris in the winter (summer, fall, spring).

When's Our Date?

No doubt, when making travel plans and arrangements, you will often have to refer to and ask for dates. The following questions will help you get the information you need about the day and the date:

What day is it (today)?
Quel jour est-ce?   Quel jour sommes-nous?
kehl zhoor ehs   *kehl zhoor sohm-noo*

What is (today's) date?
Quelle est la date (d'aujourd'hui)?
Kehl eh lah daht (do-zhoord-wee)

And the answers to these questions are:

Today is...
C'est aujourd'hui + (day) date
seh toh-zhoor-dwee

Today is...
Aujourd'hui nous sommes + (day) date
oh-zhoor-dwee noo sohm

To express dates for appointments, travel plans, and meetings in French follow these simple guidelines:

➤ Dates in French are expressed as follows:

day of week + le (cardinal) number + month + year

lundi le onze juillet dix-neuf cent quatre-vingt-dix-neuf

➤ Use *premier* to express the first of each month. Use cardinal numbers for all other days:

le premier juin	June 1st
le deux juin	June 2nd

➤ Just as in English, years are usually expressed in hundreds. When the word for *thousand* is written in dates only, *mil* is often used instead of *mille:*

1999   dix-neuf cent quatre-vingt neuf

mil neuf cent quatre-vingt neuf

Notice how the date is written in French:

French	English
le 14 septembre 1947	September 14, 1947
14.9.47	9/14/47

Remember to reverse the month/day sequence used in English.

You'll need certain time-related words and expressions when you have to make plans and schedule your time wisely. When time is of the essence, keep the expressions in Table 7.7 in mind.

Table 7.7   Time Expressions

English	French	Pronunciation
ago	il y a...	*eel yah*
the day after tomorrow	après-demain	*ah-preh duh-maN*
the day before yesterday	avant-hier	*ah-vahN yehr*
a day	un jour	*uhN zhoor*
during	pendant...	*pahN-dahN*
from	dès...	*deh*
in	dans...	*dahN*
last	dernier (dernière)	*dehr-nyah (dehr-nyehr)*
last	passé(e)	*pah-say*
a month	un mois	*uhN mwah*
the next day	le lendemain	*luh lahN-duh-maN*
next	prochain(e)	*proh-shahN (proh-shehn)*
today	aujourd'hui	*oh-zhoor-dwee*
tomorrow	demain	*duh-maN*
a week from today	d'aujourd'hui en huit	*aadoh-zhoor-dwee ahN weet*
a week	une semaine	*ewn suh-mehn*
a year	un an	*uhN nahN*
a year	une année	*ewn ah-nay*
yesterday	hier	*yehr*

Use the definite article to express *on* with dates.

Je pars le douze janvier.   I'm leaving on January 12.

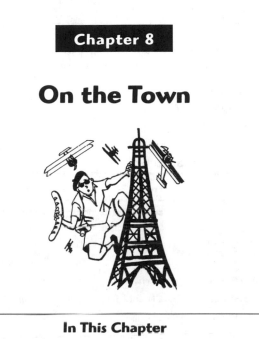

Chapter 8

On the Town

In This Chapter

➤ Sights for tourists

➤ How to make suggestions and plans

➤ How to give your opinion

It's important to plan a logical itinerary for travel in a foreign country. Group by vicinity all the important tourist attractions you want to see for the day. You wouldn't want to waste precious vacation time running back and forth across the city. The key is to have a good game plan!

With all the opportunities available to you in the French-speaking countries around the world, you'll have to decide on a daily basis if you're in the mood for sightseeing or relaxing. Does your body scream for a leisurely pace or are you raring to pack your day with as many activities as possible? The brochures that are available at airports and tourist offices will suggest many interesting and exciting things to do. Table 8.1 provides the words and phrases you need to talk about your choices.

I would like to go...
Je voudrais aller...
zhuh voo-dreh

Table 8.1 Places to Go

English	French	Pronunciation
to the amusement park	au parc d'attractions	*o pahrk dah-trahk-syohN*
to the aquarium	à l'aquarium	*a lah-kwah-ryuhm*
to the carnival	au carnaval	*o kahr-nah-vahl*
to the castle	au château	*o shah-to*
to the cathedral	à la cathédrale	*ah lah kah-tay-drahl*
to the church	à l'église	*ah lay gleez*
to the circus	au cirque	*o seerk*
to the flea market	au marché aux puces	*o mahr-shay-o pews*
to the fountain	à la fontaine	*ah lah fohn-tehn*
to the garden	au jardin	*o zhahr-daN*
to the museum	au musée	*o mew-zay*
to the nightclub	au cabaret	*o kah-bah-reh*
to the public square	à la place	*ah lah plahs*
to the zoo	au zoo	*o zo*

Seeing the Sights

Whether you decide to go it alone or opt to take a tour, the following phrases will come in handy:

Where is the tourist office?
Où est l'office du tourisme?
oo eh loh-fees dew too-ree-muh

What is there to see?
Qu'est-ce qu'il y a à voir?
kehs-keel yah ah vwahr

Where can I buy a map (a guide book)?
Où puis-je acheter une carte (un guide)?
oo pweezh ahsh-tay ewn kahrt (uhN geed)

At what time does it open (close)?
À quelle heure ouvre (ferme)-t-il?
ah kehl uhr oov-ruh (fehrm) teel?

What's the admission price?
Quel est le tarif?
kehl eh luh tah-reef

Can children enter free?
L'entrée est gratuit pour les enfants?
lahN-tray eh grah-twee poor lay zahN-fahN

Until what age?	How much do they pay?
Jusqu'à quel âge?	Ils payent combien?
zhews-kah kehl ahzh	*eel peh kohN-byaN*

Is it all right to take pictures?
On peut faire des photos?
ohN put fehr day foh-to

I need a guide who speaks English.
Il me faut un guide qui parle anglais.
eel muh fo tuhN geed kee pahrl ahN-gleh

How much does he charge?	Where are there trips?
Combien prend-il?	Où y a-t-il des visites
kohN-byaN prahN-teel	guidées?
gee-day	*oo ee yah-teel day vee-zeet*

To express what you would like to see or are going to see, you will need the irregular verb *voir* (to see) shown in Table 8.2.

Table 8.2   The Verb voir (to see)

French	Pronunciation	English
je vois	*zhuh vwah*	I see
tu vois	*tew vwah*	you see
il, elle, on voit	*eel, (ehl, ohN) vwah*	he, she, one sees
nous voyons	*noo vwah-yohN*	we see
vous voyez	*voo vwah-yay*	you see
ils, elles voient	*eel (ehl) vwah*	they see

May I Suggest

It's been your dream to see the Folies Bergères. Fascinating ads, posters, films, and pictures have enticed you and have piqued your curiosity. You don't know, however, how the others in your group feel about accompanying you. Go for it! Make the suggestion. There are two options in French that you'll find quite simple.

➤ You may use the pronoun *on* + the conjugated form of the verb that explains what it is you want to do:

On va aux Folies Bergères?
ohN vah o foh-lee behr-zhehr
How about going to the Folies Bergères?

Full Speed Ahead

With *on* use the third person singular form (il) of the verb.

➤ Another way to propose an activity is to use the command form that has **nous** as its understood subject:

Allons aux Folies Bergères!
ah-lohN zo foh-lee behr-zhehr
Let's go to the Folies Bergères!

Full Speed Ahead

When using this command form, it is unnecessary to use the subject pronoun *nous*.

➤ Try telling a friend what you'd like to do and then ask for his or her feelings about the idea.

I'd like to go the the Folies Bergères. What do you think?
Je voudrais aller aux Folies Bergères. Qu'en penses-tu?
zhuh voo-dreh-zah-lay o foh-lee behr-zhehr kahN pahNs-tew

An Extra Workout

The weather is delightful and you're eager to go out and have a great time. Suggest five things that we can do together and express each suggestion in two different ways.

Colloquially Speaking

At this point, you should be feeling rather confident about using French, so it's time to take a more sophisticated approach. There are a number of phrases you can use, all of which are followed by the infinitive of the verb (The familiar forms [tu] are in parenthesis.):

Ça vous (te) dit de...	*sah voo (tuh) dee duh*	Do you want to...
Ça vous (t')intéresse de...	*sah voozaN (taN)-tay-rehs duh*	Are you interested in...
Ça vous (te) plairait de...	*sah voo (tuh) pleh-reh duh...*	Would it please you to...
Vous voulez... (Tu veux...)	*voo voo-lay (tew vuh)*	Do you want to...

Any of the phrases listed above can be made negative by using *ne...pas:*

Ça *ne* te dit *pas* de (d')...   jouer au tennis?
(Don't you want to...?)

Ça *ne* vous intéresse *pas* de (d')...   aller au musée?
(Aren't you interested in...)

Do you know any grouchy-from-lack-of-sleep young adults who give rapid-fire yes or no answers to questions? As for the rest of us, we usually say "yes, but..." or "no, because..." In French, if you'd like to elaborate on your answer, here's what you'll have to do: Change the pronoun *vous* or *te* (*t'*) from the question to *me* (*m'*) in your answer.

Oui (Si), ça m'intéresse de (d')...   aller au musée.

Oui (Si), ça me plairait de (d')...   jouer au tennis.

Non, ça ne me dit pas de (d')...   aller au musée.

Non, je ne veux pas...   jouer au tennis.

So What Do You Think?

When you want to express a positive feeling about a suggestion that was made to you, you would say:

J'aime l'art moderne.
zhehm lahr moh-dehrn
I like modern art.

J'adore la musique.
zhah-dohr lah mew-zeek
I love music.

Je suis fana de football.
zhuh swee fah-nah duh foot-bohl
I'm crazy about soccer. (I'm a soccer freak.)

If you have the occasion to do something or go somewhere new, different, exotic, out of the ordinary, you're certainly going to have an opinion about whether you liked it or not. Is it fun? Are you having a good time? Are you amused? Give your positive opinion by saying *C'est* (*seh*—meaning "it is") + an adjective.

chouette! (*shoo-eht*)	great
extra! (*ehks-trah*)	exraordinary
formidable! (*fohr-mee-dahbl*)	great
génial! (*zhay-nyahl*)	fantastic
magnifique! (*mah-nyee-feek*)	magnificent
merveilleux! (*mehr-veh-yuh*)	marvelous
sensationnel! (*sahN-sah-syoh-nehl*)	sensational
super! (*sew-pehr*)	super
superbe! (*sew-pehrb*)	superb

Maybe the suggestion presented to you is unappealing. Perhaps you find the activity boring. To express your dislikes you might say:

Je n'aime pas l'opéra.	I don't like the opera.
Je déteste le ballet.	I hate the ballet.
Je ne suis pas fana de golf.	I'm not crazy about golf.

You wanted to be a good sport, so you tried the activity anyway. It was just as you thought: not your cup of tea. To give your negative opinion about an activity you can use *C'est* (*seh,* meaning "it is") + an adjective:

affreux (*ah-fruh*)	frightful, horrible
dégoûtant (*day-goo-tahN*)	disgusting
désagréable (*day-zah-gray-ahbl*)	unpleasant
embêtant (*ahN-beh-tahN*)	boring
ennuyeux (*ahN-nwee-yuh*)	boring
horrible (*oh-reebl*)	horrible
la barbe (*lah bahrb*)	boring
ridicule (*ree-dee-kewl*)	ridiculous

The Shopping Experience

Do you agonize over what to buy that special someone? Do you place great importance on selecting the perfect gift? Do you have endless debates with yourself over color, size, material, and design? Or do you choose the first item that strikes your fancy? Are you always in search of a bargain? How important to you is comparison shopping? Shopping doesn't have to be a chore. With a good plan of action, it can be a pleasant and an enjoyable experience for even the most crotchety among us.

You can browse in a small boutique or have the extensive selection provided by a large, elegant mall (*un centre commercial—uhN sahNtr koh-mehr-syahl*) such as le Forum des Halles in Paris or the underground Place Bonaventure in Montreal. Table 9.1 points you in the direction of stores that might interest you and the merchandise you can purchase in them.

Table 9.1   Stores (les magasins—lay mah-gah-zaN)

Store	French	Pronunciation
bookstore	la librairie	*lah lee-breh-ree*
boutique	la boutique	*lah boo-teek*
department store	le grand magasin	*luh grahN mah-gah-zaN*
florist	le magasin de fleuriste	*luh mah-gah-saN duh fluh-reest*
jewelry store	la bijouterie	*lah bee-zhoo-tree*
leather goods store	la maroquinerie	*lah mah-roh-kaN-ree*
newsstand	le kiosk à journaux	*luh kee-ohsk ah zhoor-noh*
perfume store	la parfumerie	*lah par-fewm-ree*
record store	le magasin de disques	*luh mah-gah-zaN duh deesk*
souvenir shop	le magasin de souvenirs	*luh mah-gah-zaN duh soo-neer*
tobacconist	le bureau de tabac	*luh bew-ro duh tah-bah*

Remember to save your receipts when you make purchases in any foreign country. Foreign visitors are charged a value-added tax (TVA—*taxe à la valeur ajoutée*) on certain purchases. (This tax is often 13% on a minimum purchase of 2,000F.) Some countries will return this tax (which could be considerable) upon presentation of a sales slip. Go to the specially marked windows at the airport or in large department stores to see whether any money is owed to you. Keep in mind that you might also have to pay U.S. taxes on your purchases.

General Questions

Could you please help me?
Pourriez-vous m'aider, s'il vous plaît?
poor-yay voo meh-day seel voo pleh

Would you please show me...?
Veuillez me montrer...?
vuh-yay muh mohN-tray

Are there any sales?
Y a-t-il des soldes?
ee ah-teel day sohld

Where can I find...?
Où puis-je trouver...?
oo pweezh troo-vay

Are they any discounts?
Y a-t-il des rabais?
ee ah-teel day rah-bch

Do you sell...?
Vendez-vous...?
vahN-day voo

Where is (are)...?
Où est-ce qu'il y a...?
oo ehs-keel yah

Do you have something...?
Avez-vous quelque chose...?
ah-vay voo kehl-kuh shohz

English	French	Pronunciation
else	d'autre	*do-truh*
larger	de plus grand	*duh plew grahN*
smaller	de plus petit	*duh plew puh-tee*
longer	de plus long	*duh plew lohN*
shorter	de plus court	*duh plew koor*
less expensive	de moins cher	*duh mwaN shehr*
more expensive	de plus cher	*duh plew shehr*
better	de meilleure qualité	*duh meh-yuhr kah-lee-tay*

Clothing

You simply can't take a trip to France, the fashion capital of the world, without coming home with at least one article of clothing sporting a French label. It is really *de rigueur* (duh ree-guhr) to be *dans le vent* (*dahN luh vahN*), in fashion. Table 9.2 will help you in your quest for something *au courant.*

Table 9.2   Clothing (les vêtements—lay veht-mahN)

Item of Clothing	French	Pronunciation
For One and All		
bathing suit	le maillot	*luh mah-yo*
belt	la ceinture	*lah saN-tewr*
boots	les bottes (f.)	*lay boht*
gloves	les gants (m.)	*lay gahN*
hat	le chapeau	*luh shah-po*
jacket	la veste	*lah vehst*
jeans	le jean	*luh zheen*
jogging suit	le jogging	*luh zhoh-geeng*
overcoat	le manteau	*luh mahN-to*
pants	le pantalon	*luh pahN-tah-lohN*
pajamas	le pyjama	*luh pee-zhah-mah*
raincoat	l'imperméable (m.)	*laN-pehr-may-ahbl*
robe	la robe de chambre	*lah rohb duh shahNbr*
sandals (f.)	les sandales	*lay sahN-dahl*
scarf	l'écharpe (f.), le foulard	*lay-shahrp, luh foo-lahr*
shirt	la chemise	*lah shuh-meez*
shoes	les chaussures (f.), les souliers (m.)	*lay sho-sewr, lay sool-lyay*
sneakers	les tennis	*lay tuh-nees*
socks	les chaussettes (f.)	*lay sho-seht*
umbrella	le parapluie	*luh pah-rah-plwee*
vest	le gilet	*luh zhee-leh*

Item of Clothing	French	Pronunciation
	For Men Only	
coat (sport)	la veste	*lah vehst*
shorts (undergarments)	le caleçon	*luh kahl-sohN*
suit	le complet, le costume	*luh kohN-pleh, luh kohs-tewm*
tie	la cravate	*lah krah-vaht*
undershirt	le maillot de corps	*luh mah-yod kohr*
	For Women Only	
bikini	le bikini	*luh bee-kee-nee*
(string) bikini	la ficelle	*lah fee-sehl*
brassière	le soutien-gorge	*luh soo-tyaN gohrzh*
blouse	le chemisier, la blouse	*luh shuh-meez-yay, lah blooz*
dress	la robe	*lah rohb*
negligee	le peignoir	*luh peh-nywahr*
panties	la culotte	*lah kew-loht*
pantyhose (tights)	le collant	*luh koh-lahN*
pocketbook	le sac (à main)	*luh sahk (ah maN)*
skirt	la jupe	*lah zhewp*
slip (half), (full)	le jupon, la combinaison	*luh zhew-pohN, lah kohN-bee-neh-sohN*
stockings	les bas (m.)	*lay bah*
suit	le tailleur	*luh tah-yuhr*

Of course you want to make sure you wind up with items that fit right. Tell the salesperson the following:

I wear...	small	medium	large
Je porte du...	petit	moyen	grand
zhuh pohrt dew	*puh-tee*	*mwah-yaN*	*grahN*

For shoes you would say:

> I wear shoe size…
> Je chausse du… + size
> *zhuh shohs dew*

Colors

Do you see the world in primary colors? Or do you tend to go for the more exotic, artistic shades? Table 9.3 will help you learn the basic colors so you can get by.

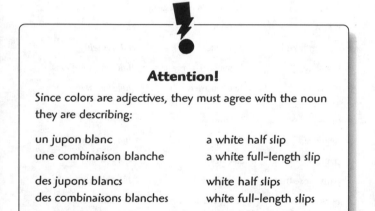

Attention!

Since colors are adjectives, they must agree with the noun they are describing:

un jupon blanc	a white half slip
une combinaison blanche	a white full-length slip
des jupons blancs	white half slips
des combinaisons blanches	white full-length slips

Table 9.3 Colors (les couleurs—lay koo-luhr)

Color	French	Color	French
black	noir(e) (*nwahr*)	blue	bleu(e) (*bluh*)
brown	brun(e) (*bruhN, brewn*)	gray	gris(e) (*gree[z]*)
green	vert(e) (*vehr[t]*)	orange	orange (*oh-rahNzh*)
pink	rose (*roz*)	purple	mauve (*mov*)
red	rouge (*roozh*)	white	blanc(he) (*blahN[sh]*)
yellow	jaune (*zhon*)		

Full Speed Ahead

To describe a color as *light* add the word *clair*.
To describe a color as *dark* add the word *foncé*.

light blue	*bleu clair*
dark green	*vert foncé*

Materials

Did you even unpack only to wish you had brought along a travel iron? Or do you hang your wrinkled garments in a steamy, humid bathroom hoping for the best? Will you only go with permanent press or do you prefer richer materials that will give you a more worldly, sophisticated look? If you expect to make a clothing purchase while on vacation, Table 9.4 will help you select the material you prefer for your special wants and needs. Use the word *en* (*ahN*) to express "in."

Table 9.4   Materials (les tissus—*lay tee-sew*)

Material	French	Pronunciation
cashmere	en cachemire	*ahN kahsh-meer*
corduroy	en velours côtelée	*ahN vuh-loor koht-lay*
cotton	en coton	*ahN koh-tohN*
denim	en jean	*ahN zheen*
flannel	en flanelle	*ahN flah-nehl*
lace	en dentelle	*ahN dahN-tehl*
leather	en cuir	*ahN kweer*

continues

Table 9.4   Continued

Material	French	Pronunciation
linen	en lin	*ahN laN*
nylon	en nylon	*ahN nee-lohN*
polyester	en polyester	*ahN poh-lee-ehs-tehr*
silk	en soie	*ahN swah*
suede	en daim	*ahN daN*
terry cloth	en tissu éponge	*ahN tee-sew ay-pohNzh*
velvet	en velours	*ahN vuh-loor*
wool	en laine	*ahN lehn*

Read the Labels

Do you remember the time you accidentally put your favorite 100% wool sweater in the washing machine? Make sure to read all labels carefully for the following information:

non-shrinkable	non-rétrécissable	*nohN-ray-tray-see-sahbl*
washable	lavable	*lah-vahbl*
wrinkle-resistant	en tissu infroissable	*ahN tee-sew aN-frwah-sahbl*

Use the irregular verb *mettre* in Table 9.5 to express what clothing you put on:

Table 9.5   The Verb mettre (to put on)

French	Pronunciation	English
je mets	*zhuh meh*	I put (on)
tu mets	*tew meh*	you put (on)
il met	*eel meh*	he puts (on)

French	Pronunciation	English
nous mettons	*noo meh-tohN*	we put (on)
vous mettez	*voo meh-tay*	you put (on)
ils mettent	*eel meht*	they put (on)

Designs

Suppose you're on the hunt for a chic sweater you saw in the latest fashion magazine. Or maybe you'd like a plaid pair of golf pants because you really want to stand out. Or perhaps you're not even into shopping, but you'd like to compliment someone on the good taste of his striped tie. Table 9.6 provides the words you need to describe patterns.

Table 9.6   Designs (le dessins—luh deh-saN)

Design	French	Pronunciation
in a solid color	uni(e)	*ew-nee*
with stripes	à rayures	*ah rah-yewr*
with polka dots	à pois	*ah pwah*
in plaid	en tartan	*ahN tahr-tahN*
in herringbone	à chevrons	*ah shuh-vrohN*
checked	à carreaux	*ah kah-ro*

Object Pronouns

Object pronouns replace direct and indirect object nouns to avoid the constant monotonous repetition of a word.

Direct objects (which can be nouns or pronouns) answer the question **whom** or **what** the subject is acting upon and may refer to people, places, things, or ideas.

Indirect objects answer the question *to* whom the subject is doing something or *for* whom the subject is acting. Indirect objects only refer to people.

Direct and indirect object nouns may be replaced by the pronouns in Table 9.7.

Table 9.7 Direct and Indirect Object Pronouns

Direct Object Pronouns			Indirect Object Pronouns		
me (m')	*muh*	me	me (m')	*muh*	(to) me
te (t')	*tuh*	you (familiar)	te (t')	*tuh*	(to) you (familiar)
le (l')	*luh*	he, it	lui	*lwee*	(to) him
la (l')	*lah*	her, it	lui	*lwee*	(to) her
nous	*noo*	us	nous	*noo*	(to) us
vous	*voo*	you (polite)	vous	*voo*	(to) you
les	*lay*	them	leur	*luhr*	(to) them

The French preposition *à (au, à la, à l', aux)* followed by the name of or reference to a person indicates that an indirect object is needed. Some verbs like *répondre (à)*, *téléphoner (à)*, and *ressembler (à)* are always followed by *à* + person and will, therefore, always take an indirect object pronoun.

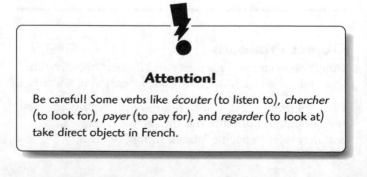

Attention!

Be careful! Some verbs like *écouter* (to listen to), *chercher* (to look for), *payer* (to pay for), and *regarder* (to look at) take direct objects in French.

Object pronouns are placed before the verb to which their meaning is tied (usually the conjugated verb).

Il *la* prend.	Tu ne vas pas *lui* parler.
He takes it.	You aren't going to speak to him/her.

Full Speed Ahead

Read the following two sentences:

I write (to) her a post card.

I bought (for) him a car.

In English, the **to** or **for** is often understood, but not used. So be careful in French when choosing a direct or indirect object pronoun.

Asking for What You Want

We've all had an experience with a salesperson hovering over us greedily anticipating making a huge sale. Don't they understand that sometimes we just want to browse? At other times, however, we have specific wants and needs and require assistance. Here are some phrases to help you deal with most common situations.

Questions a store an employee might ask you:

Puis-je vous aider?	Vous désirez?
pweezh voo zeh-day	*voo day-zee-ray*
May I help you?	

Just looking? Then you would answer:

No, thank you, I am (just) looking.
Non, merci, je regarde (tout simplement).
nohN mehr-see zhuh ruh-gahrd (too saN-pluh-mahN)

If you want to see or buy something, you would answer:

Yes, I would like to see…please.
Oui, je voudrais voir…s'il vous plaît.
wee zhuh voo-dreh vwahr…seel voo pleh

I'm looking for…
Je cherche…
zhuh shehrsh

And of course, if you're a shopper like I am, you'd want to know:

Are there any sales?	Have you slashed your prices?
Y a-t-il des soldes?	Avez-vous cassé les prix?
ee yah teel day sohld	*ah-vay-voo kah-say lay pree*

Preferences

When the salesperson wants to help you make a choice expect to hear:

Which shirt do you prefer?
Quelle chemise est-ce que vous préférez?
kehl shuh-meez esh-kuh voo pray-fay-ray

Full Speed Ahead

To express "which one?", use an interrogative adjective, which must agree with the noun to which it refers:

	Masculine	Feminine
Singular	lequel (*luh-kehl*)	laquelle (*lah-kehl*)
Plural	lesquels (*lay-kehl*)	lesquelles (*lay-kehl*)

Expressing Yourself

Girl, were you poured into those pants? That dress is you! What an adorable hat! To express your pleasure when you are satisfied with an item say one of the following:

I like it.	Ça me plaît.	*sah muh pleh*
It suits (fits) me.	Ça me va.	*sah muh vah*
It's nice.	C'est agréable.	*seh tah-gray-ahbl*
It's elegant.	C'est élégant(e).	*seh tay-lay-gahN*

If you're dissatisfied, you might use the following:

I don't like it.	Ça ne me plaît pas.	*sah nuh muh pleh pah*
It doesn't suit (fit) me.	Ça ne me va pas.	*sah nuh muh vah pah*
It's horrible.	C'est abominable.	*seh tah-boh-mee-nahbl*
It's too small.	C'est trop petit(e).	*seh tro puh-tee(t)*
It's too tight.	C'est trop serré(e).	*seh tro suh-ray*
It's too short.	C'est trop court(e).	*seh tro koor(t)*
It's too long.	C'est trop long(ue).	*seh tro lohN(g)*
It's too loud.	C'est trop criard(e).	*seh tro kree-ahr*
It's too narrow.	C'est trop étroit(e).	*seh tro pay-trwaht*

If you're not satisfied and want something else:

I'm looking for something more (less)...
Je cherche quelque chose de plus (moins) + adjective
zhuh shehrsh kehl kuh shooz duh plew (mwaN)

Use a demonstrative adjective to express this, that, these, or those.

used before masculine singular nouns beginning with a consonant	used before masculine singular nouns beginning with a vowel	used before all feminine singular nouns	used before all plural nouns
ce (*suh*)	cet (*seht*)	cette (*seht*)	ces (*say*)
ce pantalon	cet imperméable	cette écharpe	ces imperméables
		cette jupe	ces jupes

Demonstrative adjectives precede the nouns they modify and agree with them in number and gender. The special masculine form *cet* is used to prevent a clash of two vowel sounds together.

An Extra Workout

Open a magazine. Describe and then comment upon all the clothing you see. Give both positive and negative opinions.

Chapter 10

Food, Glorious Food

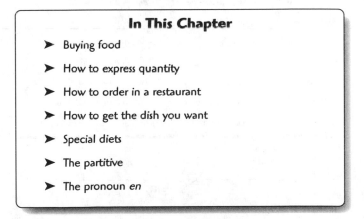

In This Chapter

➤ Buying food

➤ How to express quantity

➤ How to order in a restaurant

➤ How to get the dish you want

➤ Special diets

➤ The partitive

➤ The pronoun *en*

Whether you make reservations in a swanky four-star restaurant or just stop by a local *charcuterie (shahr-kew-tree*—deli) to prick up a bite to tide you over, you need to know how to ask for the foods you want and how to refuse those that don't have any appeal. You'll also want to make sure you order the proper quantity. All your dietary cravings will be satisfied in this chapter.

Specialty Shops

First thing I do when I get to a foreign country is scout out the nearest food store, just in case I develop a severe case of the midnight munchies. In any French-speaking country you can enjoy the culinary delights that can be purchased in the shops listed in Table 10.1

Table 10.1 Food Shops

English	French	Pronunciation
bakery	une boulangerie	*ewn boo-lahNzh-ree*
butcher shop	une boucherie	*ewn boosh-ree*
candy store	une confiserie	*ewn kohN-feez-ree*
dairy store	une crémerie	*ewn kraym-ree*
delicatessen	une charcuterie	*ewn shahr-keww-tree*
fruit store	une fruiterie	*ewn frwee-tree*
grocery store	une épicerie	*ewn ay-pees-ree*
pastry shop	une pâtisserie	*ewn pah-tees-ree*
fish store	une poissonnerie	*ewn pwah-sohn-ree*
liquor store	un magasin de vins	*uhN mah-gah-zaN duh vaN*
supermarket	un supermarché	*uhN sew-pehr-mahr-shay*

Full Speed Ahead

Many of the names of the stores end in **-erie**. Drop this ending and add **-ier (-ière)** to get the name of the male (female) person who works in the store.

Full Speed Ahead

It is very common to use the preposition *chez* (to [at] the house [business] of) + the person to express where you are going:

➤ Je vais chez l'épicier (épicière).

➤ Je vais chez le (la) boulanger (boulangère).

Food and More Food

Knowing the French names of the foods you like and dislike will put you at a distinct advantage whether you're in a store or at a restaurant. Use Tables 10.2–10.9 to pick and choose at will

Table 10.2   At the Grocery Store

Vegetables	Les Légumes	*lay lay-gewm*
asparagus	les asperges (f.)	*lay zahs-pehrzh*
beans (green)	les haricots (m.) (verts)	*lay zah-ree-koh (vehr)*
broccoli	le brocoli	*luh broh-koh-lee*
carrot	le carotte	*luh kah-roht*
celery	le céleri	*luh sehl-ree*
cauliflower	le chou-fleur	*luh shoo-fluhr*
cucumber	le concombre	*luh kohN-kohNbr*
corn	le maïs	*luh mah-ees*
eggplant	l'aubergine	*lo-behr-zheen*
lettuce	la laitue	*lah leh-tew*

continues

Table 10.2 Continued

Vegetables	Les Légumes	*lay lay-gewm*
mushroom	le champignon	*luh shahN-pee-nyohN*
onion	l'oignon	*loh-nyohN*
peas	les petits pois (m.)	*lay puh-tee pwah*
pepper	le piment, le poivron	*luh pee-mahN, luh pwah-vrohN*
potato	la pomme de terre	*lah pohm duh tehr*
rice	le riz	*luh ree*
spinach	les épinards (m.)	*lay zay-pee-nahr*
tomato	la tomate	*lah toh-maht*

Table 10.3 At the Fruit Store

Fruits	Les Fruits	*lay frwee*
apple	la pomme	*lah pohm*
apricot	l'abricot (m.)	*lah-bree-ko*
banana	la banane	*lah bah-nahn*
blueberry	la myrtille	*lah meer-tee-y*
cherry	la cerise	*lah suh-reez*
coconut	la noix de coco	*lah nwah duh koh-ko*
grape	le raisin	*luh reh-zahN*
grapefruit	le pamplemousse	*luh pahNpl-moos*
lemon	le citron	*luh see-trohN*
lime	le citron vert	*luh see-trohN vehr*
orange	l'orange (f.)	*loh-rahNzh*
peach	la pêche	*lah pehsh*
pear	la poire	*lah pwahr*
pineapple	l'ananas (m.)	*lah-nah-nah*
plum	la prune	*lah prewn*

Fruits	Les Fruits	*lay frwee*
prune	le pruneau	*luh prew-no*
raisin	le raisin sec	*luh reh-zaN sehk*
raspberry	la framboise	*lah frahN-bwahz*
strawberry	la fraise	*lah frehz*
tangerine	la mandarine	*lah mahN-dah-reen*
watermelon	la pastèque	*lah pahs-tehk*

Table 10.4   At the Butcher or Delicatessen

Meats	Les Viandes	*lay vyahNd*
beef	le boeuf	*luh buhf*
chopped meat	la viande hachée	*lah vyahNd ah-shay*
ham	le jambon	*luh zhahN-bohN*
lamb	l'agneau (m.)	*lah-nyo*
liver	le foie	*luh fwah*
pork	le porc	*luh pohr*
roast beef	le rosbif	*luh rohs-beef*
sausage	les saucisses (f.)	*lay so-sees*
spareribs	les basses côtes (f.)	*lay bahs kot*
stew	le ragoût	*luh rah-goo*
tongue	la langue	*lah lahNg*
veal	le veau	*luh vo*

Fowl/Game	La Volaille/Le Gibier	*lah voh-lahy/luh zhee-byay*
chicken	le poulet	*luh poo-leh*
duck	le canard	*luh kah-nard*
goose	l'oie (f.)	*lwah*
rabbit	le lapin	*luh lah-paN*

continues

Table 10.4 Continued

Fowl/Game	La Volaille/Le Gibier	*lah voh-lahy/luh zhee-byay*
turkey	la dinde	*lah daNd*
venison	la venaison	*lah vuh-neh-zohN*

Full Speed Ahead

Thicker than our traditional meat loaf, pâté is a liver paste. Although usually made with goose; duck, pork, or chicken may be used instead. Wine is an essential ingredient to the ground meat mixture. The pâté is baked in a loaf, then allowed to cool. It is served cold, often with bread or crackers. Pâté is sometimes baked in a decorated pastry crust (*en croûte—ahN kroot*), which lends it additional flavor.

Table 10.5 At the Fish Store

Fish/Seafood	Le Poisson/Les Fruits de Mer	*luh pwah-sohN/lay frweed mehr*
bass	la perche	*lah pehrsh*
clam	la palourde	*lah pah-loord*
codfish	le cabillaud	*lah kah-bee-yo*
crab	le crabe	*luh krahb*
flounder	le carrelet	*luh kahr-leh*
frogs' legs	les cuisses de grenouille (f.)	*lay kwees duh gruh-nuhy*
grouper	le mérou	*luh may-roo*

Fish/Seafood	Le Poisson/Les Fruits de Mer	*luh pwah-sohN/lay frweed mehr*
halibut	le flétan	*luh flay-tahN*
herring	le hareng	*luh ah-rahN*
lobster	le homard	*luh oh-mahr*
mackerel	le maquereau	*luh mahk-roh*
monkfish	la lotte	*lah loht*
mussel	la moule	*lah mool*
oyster	l'huître	*lwee-truh*
red snapper	la perche rouge	*lah pehrsh roozh*
salmon	le saumon	*luh so-mohN*
sardine	la sardine	*luh sahr-deen*
scallops	les coquilles	*lay koh-kee*
sea bass	le bar	*luh bahr*
shrimp	la crevette	*lah kruh-veht*
snail	l'escargot (m.)	*lehs-kahr-go*
sole	la sole	*lah sohl*
squid	le calmar	*luh kahl-mahr*
swordfish	l'espadon	*lehs-pah-dohN*
trout	la truite	*lah trweet*
tuna	le thon	*luh tohN*

Table 10.6 At the Dairy

Dairy Products	Produits Laitiers	*proh-dwee leh-tyeh*
butter	le beurre	*luh buhr*
cheese	le fromage	*luh froh-mahzh*
cream	la crème	*lah krehm*
eggs	des oeufs (m.)	*day zuh*
yogurt	le yaourt	*luh yah-oort*

Table 10.7   At the Bakery and Pastry Shop

Breads/Desserts	Pains/Desserts	*paN/duh-sehr*
apple turnover	le chausson aux pommes	*luh sho-sohN o pohm*
bread	le pain	*luh paN*
cake	le gâteau	*luh gah-to*
cookie	le biscuit	*luh bees-kwee*
cream puffs	les choux à la crème (m.)	*lay shoo ah lah krehm*
crescent roll	le croissant	*luh krwah-sahN*
danish	la danoise	*lah dah-nwahz*
doughnut	le beignet	*luh beh-nyeh*
French bread	la baguette	*lah bah-geht*
pie	la tarte	*lah tahrt*
roll	le petit pain	*luh puh-tee paN*

Table 10.8   At the Candy Store

Sweets	Les Sucreries	*lay sew-kreh-ree*
candy	les bonbons (m.)	*lay bohN-bohN*
chocolate	le chocolat	*luh shoh-koh-lah*

Table 10.9   At the Beverage Counter

Drinks	Les Boissons	*lay bwah-sohN*
beer	la bière	*lah byehr*
champagne	le champagne	*luh shahN-pah-nyuh*
coffee	le café	*luh kah-fay*
juice	le jus	*luh zhew*
lemonade	le citron pressé	*lun see-trohN preh-say*

Drinks	Les Boissons	*lay bwah-sohN*
milk	le lait	*luh leh*
mineral water carbonated non-carbonated	l'eau minérale (f.) gazeuse plate	*lo mee-nay-rahl gah-zuhz pluht*
tea	le thé	*luh tay*
wine	le vin	*luh vaN*

Getting the Right Amount

In France, the metric system is used for measuring quantities of food. Solids are measured in kilograms or fractions thereof, and liquids are measured in liters. Most of us are used to measuring in ounces, pounds, pints, quarts, and gallons. The following convenient conversion chart in Table 10.10 will help you get the hand of the metric system.

Table 10.10   Measuring Quantities of Food

Approximate Solid Measures

1 oz. = 28 grams	¾ lb. = 375 grams
¼ lb. = 125 grams	1.1 lb. = 500 grams
½ lb. = 250 grams	2.2 lb. = 1000 grams (1 kilogram)
1 oz. = 30 milliliters	16 oz. (1 pint) = 475 milliliters
32 oz. (1 quart) = 950 milliliters (approximately 1 liter)	1 gallon = 3.75 liters

The metric system is a complete mystery to me. So if, like me, you're a bit confused, Table 10.11 should make it even easier for you. Sometimes just asking for a box, bag, jar, etc. is easier. I suggest you memorize the amounts you're accustomed to: a pound, a quart, etc.

Table 10.11 Getting the Right Amount

English	French	Pronunciation
a bag of	un sac de	*uhN sahk duh*
a bar of	une tablette de	*ewn tah-bleht duh*
a bottle of	une bouteille de	*ewn boo-tehy duh*
a box of	une boîte de	*ewn bwaht duh*
a can of	une boîte de	*ewn bwaht duh*
a dozen	une douzaine de	*ewn doo-zehn duh*
a half pound of	deux cent cinquante grammes de	*duh sahN saN-kahNt grahm duh*
a jar of	un bocal de	*uhN boh-kahl duh*
a package of	un paquet de	*uhN pah-keh duh*
a piece of	un morceau de	*uhN mohr-so duh*
a pound of	un demi-kilo de	*uhN duh-mee kee-lo duh*
2 pounds of	un kilo de	*uhN kee-lo duh*
a quart of	un litre de	*uhN lee-truh duh*
a slice of	une tranche de	*ewn trahNsh duh*

All of these expressions of quantity include the word *de* (of). Before a vowel *de* becomes *d'*. In all other instances, *de* never changes:

> beaucoup de bonbons   a lot of candies
>
> une douzaine d'oeufs   a dozen eggs

You really want to sample that chocolate marquise your French cousin has prepared. You know the caloric content is high, but you long to savor its creamy, chocolately texture. Your cousin wants to give you more than "just a taste." Here are some expressions that will help you limit the amount you receive.

| little | un peu de | *uhN puh duh* |
| t of | beaucoup de | *bo-koo duh* |

| enough | assez de | *ah-say duh* |
| too much | trop de | *tro duh* |

Making Purchases

Be prepared for the questions that you might be asked when shopping and the proper way to give a satisfactory answer:

What would you like?	May I help you?
Vous désirez?	Est-ce que je peux vous aider?
voo day-zee-ray	*ehs-kuh zhuh puh voo zeh-day*

Your answer might begin:

I would like...	Could you give me...? please
Je voudrais...	Pourriez-vous me donner...?
zhuh voo-dreh	s'il vous plaît
	poo-ryay voo muh doh-nay
	seel voo pleh

An Extra Workout

You're on your own. Tell a shopkeeper that you would like the following: a pound of ham, a liter of soda, a chocolate bar, a box of cookies, a bag of candy, a half pound of turkey.

It's Mealtime

If you're going to eat in a restaurant, it might be necessary to reserve a table. When you call, make sure to include all the pertinent information, as follows:

I would like to reserve a table…
Je voudrais réserver une table…
zhuh voo-dreh ray-sehr-vay ewn tahbl

for this evening	for tomorrow evening
pour ce soir	pour demain soir
poor suh swahr	*poor duh-maN swahr*
for Saturday night	for two people
pour samedi soir	pour deux personnes
poor sahm-dee swahr	*poor duh pehr-sohn*
at 8:30 p.m.	on the terrace, please
à huit heures et demie	(outdoors)
plaît.	sur (à) la terrasse, s'il vous
ah wee tuhr ay duh-mee	*sewr (ah) lah teh-rahs seel voo pleh*

There are a wide variety of eating establishments to accommodate your hunger and your pocketbook, whether you are you going out for breakfast (le petit déjeuner, *luh puh-tee day-zhuh-nay*), lunch (le déjeuner, *luh day-zhuh-nay*), dinner (le dîner, *luh dee-nay*), or an early afternoon snack (le goûter, *luh goo-tay*). If you're not in the mood for a formal restaurant, why not try:

➤ une auberge (*ewn o-behrzh*), an inn

➤ un bistro (*uhN bees-tro*), a small informal neighborhood pub or tavern

➤ une brasserie (*ew brahs-ree*), a large café serving quick meals

➤ une cabaret (*ewn kah-bah-reh*), a nightclub

➤ un café (*uhN kah-fay*), a small neighborhood restaurant where residents socialize

➤ un cafétéria (*uhN kah-fay-tay-ryah*), a self-service restaurant

➤ une casse-croûte (*ewn kahs-kroot*), a restaurant serving sandwiches

➤ une crêperie (*ewn krehp-ree*), a stand or restaurant serving *crêpes* (filled pancakes)

➤ un fast-food (*uhN fahst-food*), a fast food chain restaurant

➤ un self (*uhN sehlf*), a self-service restaurant

You've been seated and you're ready to eat. But wait! Monsieur's place is missing something. Table 10.12 gives you the vocabulary you need when asking the waiter for cutlery, as well as other terms that will come in handy.

Table 10.12   A Table Setting

Table Setting	Le Couvert	*luh koo-vehr*
bowl	le bol	*luh bohl*
cup	la tasse	*lah tahss*
dinner plate	l'assiette (f.)	*lah-syeht*
fork	la fourchette	*lah foor-sheht*
glass	le verre	*luh vehr*
knife	le couteau	*luh koo-to*
menu	le menu, la carte	*luh muh-new, lah kahrt*
napkin	la serviette	*lah sehr-vyeht*
pepper shaker	la poivrière	*lah pwah-vree-yehr*
place setting	le couvert	*luh koo-vehr*
salt shaker	la salière	*lah sahl-yehr*
saucer	la soucoupe	*lah soo-koop*
soup dish	l'assiette à soupe(f.)	*lah-syeht ah soop*
soup spoon	la cuiller à soupe	*lah kwee-yehr ah soop*
tablecloth	la nappe	*lah nahp*
teaspoon	la cuiller	*lah kwee-yehr*
wine glass	le verre à vin	*luh vehr ah vaN*

An Extra Workout

Ask your server for a pepper shaker, a glass, a fork, a soup spoon, a cup, and a saucer. Use *Il me faut (eel muh fo)* to express your needs.

What Do You Recommend?

Use the following questions and phrases for ordering both your drinks and your food:

What is today's specialty?
Quelle est la spécialité du jour?
kehl eh lah spay-see-yah-lee-tay dew zhoor

What is the house specialty?
Quelle est la spécialité de la maison?
kehl eh lah spay-see-yah-lee-tay duh lah meh-sohN

What do you recommend?
Qu'est-ce que vous recommandez?
kehs-kuh voo ruh-koh-mahN-day

I would like...	I'll have...
Je voudrais...	Je prendrai...
zhuh voo-dreh	*zhuh prahN-dray*

Please bring me...
Apportez-moi, s'il vous plaît...
ah-pohr-tay mwah seel voo pleh

I Need an Explanation

Are you confused and overwhelmed by the culinary terms on a French menu? The waiter will probably get lost in his explanation. Table 10.13 gives you the terms you need to know.

Table 11.13 What's on the Menu?

French	Pronunciation	Description
ailoli	*ah-yoh-lee*	mayonnaise flavored with garlic
à la bonne femme	*ah lah bohn fahm*	a white wine sauce with vegetables
béarnaise	*bay-ahr-nehz*	a butter-egg sauce flavored with wine, shallots, and tarragon
bercy	*behr-see*	a meat or fish sauce
blanquette	*blahN-keht*	a creamy egg and white wine sauce usually served with stew
crécy	*kray-see*	carrots
daube	*dohb*	a stew, usually beef, with red wine, onions, and garlic
farci(e)	*fahr-see*	a stuffing
florentine	*floh-rahN-teen*	spinach
forestière	*foh-rehs-tyehr*	wild mushrooms
hollandaise	*oh-lahN-dehz*	an egg yolk, butter sauce with lemon juice or vinegar
jardinière	*zhahr-dee-nyehr*	vegetables
maître d'hôtel	*mehtr do-tehl*	a butter sauce with parsley and lemon juice
mornay	*mohr-nay*	a white sauce with cheese
parmentier	*pahr-mahN-tyay*	potatoes
périgourdine	*pay-ree-goor-deen*	mushrooms (truffles)
provençale	*proh-vahN-sahl*	a vegetable garnish
rémoulade	*ray-moo-lahd*	mayonnaise flavored with mustard
véronique	*vay-rohN-neek*	grapes
vol-au-vent	*vohl-o-vahN*	puff pastry with creamed meat

Tables 10.14 through 10.16 will help you get from the appetizer through the main course. If you have any problems with the names of various types of meat or fish, refer back to Table 10.4.

Table 10.14   Appetizers

Les Hors-d'oeuvres	*lay zohr-duhvr*	Description
le tournedos	*luh toor-nuh-do*	small fillets of beef
les côtes de crudités variées	*krew-dee-tay vah-ryay*	sliced raw vegetables usually in a vinaigrette sauce
escargots à la bourguignonne	*ehs-kahr-go ah lah boor-gee-nyohn*	snails in garlic sauce
foie gras	*fwah grah*	fresh, sometimes uncooked goose liver, served with toasted French bread
pâté	*pah-tay*	pureed liver or other meat served in a loaf
quiche lorraine	*keesh loh-rehn*	egg custard tart served with meat (bacon or ham)
quenelles	*kuh-nehl*	dumplings
rillettes	*ree-yeht*	pork mixture served as a spread

Table 10.15   Soups

Les Soupes	*lay soop*	Description
la bisque	*lah beesk*	creamy soup made with crayfish
la bouillabaisse	*lah boo-yah-behs*	seafood stew
le consommé	*luh kohN-soh-may*	clear broth
la petite marmite	*lah puh-teet mahr-meet*	rich consommé served with vegetables and meat
le potage	*luh poh-tahzh*	thick soup made of pureed vegetables

Les Soupes	*lay soop*	Description
la soupe à l'oignon	*lah soop ah loh-nyohN*	onion soup served with bread and cheese
velouté	*vuh-loo-tay*	creamy soup

Table 10.16 Meats

Les Viandes	*lay vyahnd*	Description
le bifteck	*luh beef-tehk*	steak
l'entrecôte (f.)	*lahNtr-koht*	sirloin steak
l'escalope (f.)	*leh-skah-lohp*	scallopine, cutlet
la côte de boeuf	*lah koht duh buhf*	prime rib
la poitrine de...	*lah pwah-treen duh*	breast of...
le carré d'agneau	*luh kah-ray dah-nyo*	rack of lamb
le chateaubriand	*luh shah-to-bree-yahN*	a porterhouse steak
le foie	*luh foie*	liver
le gigot d'agneau	*luh zhee-go dah-nyo*	leg of lamb
le pot-au-feu	*luh poh-to-fuh*	boiled beef
le rosbif	*luh rohs-beef*	roast beef
les côtes de porc (f.)	*lay koht duh pohr*	pork chops
les côtes de veau (f.)	*lay koht duh vo*	veal chops
les médaillons de...(m)	*lay may-dah-yohN duh*	small rounds of...
les saucisses (f.)	*lay so-sees*	sausages

Proper Preparation

Of course, you want to make sure your meal is cooked just the way you like it. The waiter may ask the following:

How do you want it (them)?
Vous le (la, les) voulez comment?
voo luh (lah, lay) voo-lay koh-mahN

Table 10.17 will help you to express your wants and needs.

Table 10.17   How Would You Like It Prepared?

English	French	Pronunciation
Meats and Vegetables		
baked	cuit au four	*kwee to foor*
broiled	rôti	*ro-tee*
boiled	bouilli	*boo-yee*
browned	gratiné	*grah-tee-nay*
breaded	au gratin	*o grah-taN*
chopped	hâché	*ah-shay*
fried	frit	*free*
sauteed	sauté	*so-tay*
grilled	grillé	*gree-yay*
steamed	à la vapeur	*ah lah vah-puhr*
in its natural juices	au jus	*o zhew*
stewed	en cocotte	*ahN koh-koht*
mashed	en purée	*ahN pew-ray*
poached	poché	*poh-shay*
pureed	en purée	*ahN pew-ray*
roasted	rôti	*ro-tee*
very rare	bleu	*bluh*
rare	saignant	*seh-nyahN*
medium	à point	*ah pwaN*
well-done	bien cuit	*byaN kwee*
with sauce	en sauce	*ahN sos*
Eggs		
fried	au plat	*o plah*
hard-boiled	durs	*dewr*
medium-boiled	mollets	*moh-leh*
poached	pochés	*poh-shay*
scrambled	brouillés	*broo-yay*

English	French	Pronunciation
soft-boiled	à la coque	*ah lah kohk*
omelette	une omelette	*ewn nohm-leht*
plain omelette	une omelette nature	*ewn nohm-leht nah-tewr*

Full Speed Ahead

If you are very determined to have your meat prepared the way you like it, understand that French chefs have a different interpretation of the terms rare, medium, and well-done. Rare means almost alive, medium is a tiny bit more than our rare, and well done is a bit more than our medium. What the chef thinks is burned, is what we mean by well-done. He(She) may prepare it well-done, but don't expect a smile when it is served.

I Like It Spicy

Lots of herbs, spices, seasonings, and condiments are used to flavor French foods. Depend on menu descriptions or your server to help you determine whether the dish will be to your liking—bland or spicy. Table 10.18 will help you with the spices you might encounter.

Table 10.18   Herbs, Spices, and Condiments

Herbs, Spices and Condiments	Les Herbes, Les Épices et Les Condiments	*lay zehrb, lay zay-pees ay lay kohn-dee-mahn*
basil	le basilic	*luh bah-zee-leek*
bay leaf	la feuille de laurier	*lah fuhy duh loh-ryay*

continues

Table 10.18   Continued

Herbs, Spices and Condiments	Les Herbes, Les Épices et Les Condiments	*lay zehrb, lay zay-pees ay lay kohn-dee-mahn*
butter	le beurre	*luh buhr*
chives	la ciboulette	*lah see-boo-leht*
dill	l'aneth (m.)	*lah-neht*
garlic	l'ail (m.)	*lahy*
ginger	le gingembre	*luh zhaN-zhahNbr*
honey	le miel	*luh myehl*
horseradish	le raifort	*luh reh-fohr*
jam, jelly	la confiture	*lah kohN-fee-tewr*
ketchup	le ketchup	*luh keht-chuhp*
lemon	le citron	*luh see-trohN*
maple syrup	le sirop d'érable	*luh see-roh day-rahbl*
mayonnaise	la mayonnaise	*lah mah-yoh-nehz*
mint	la menthe	*lah mahNt*
mustard	la moutarde	*lah moo-tahrd*
oil	l'huile (f.)	*lweel*
oregano	l'origan (m.)	*loh-ree-gahN*
parsley	le persil	*luh pehr-seel*
pepper	le poivre	*luh pwahvr*
salt	le sel	*luh sehl*
sugar	le sucre	*luh sewkr*
tarragon	l'estragon (m.)	*lehs-trah-gohN*
vinegar	le vinaigre	*luh vee-nehgr*

Special Requests

Keep the following phrases handy if you have certain likes and dislikes, or dietary restrictions that you would like to make known:

I am on a diet.
Je suis au régime.
zhuh swee zo ray-zheem

I'm a vegetarian.
Je suis végétarien(ne).
zhuh swee vay-zhay-tah-ryaN (ryen)

I can't eat anything made with...
Je ne peux rien manger de cuisiné au (à la)...
zhuh nuh puh ryaN mahN-zhay duh kwee-zee-nay o (ah lah)

I can't have...
Je ne tolère...
zhuh nuh toh-lehr

English	French	Pronunciation
any dairy products	aucun produit laitier	*o-kuhN proh-dwee leh-tyay*
any alcohol	aucun produit alcoolique	*o-kuhN proh-dwee ahl-koh-leek*
any saturated fats	aucune matière grasse animale	*o-kewn mah-tyehr grahs ah-nee-mahl*
any shellfish	aucun fruit de mer	*o-kuhN frweed mehr*

I'm looking for a dish...
Je cherche un plat...
zhuh shehrsh uhN plah

English	French	Pronunciation
high in fiber	riche en fibre	*reesh ahN feebr*
low in cholesterol	léger en cholestérol	*lay-zhay ahN koh-lehs-tay-rohl*
low in fat	léger en matières grasses	*lay-zhay ahN mah-tyehr grahs*
low in sodium	léger en sodium	*lay-zhay ahN sohd-yuhm*
non-dairy	non-laitier	*nohN-leh-tyay*
salt-free	sans sel	*sahN sehl*

continues

continued

English	French	Pronunciation
sugar-free	sans sucre	*sahN sewkr*
without artificial coloring	sans colorant	*sahN koh-loh-rahN*
without preservatives	sans conservateurs	*sahN kohN-sehr-vah-tuhr*

Back It Goes

At times the cooking or the table setting might not up to your standards. Table 10.19 presents some problems you might encounter.

Table 10.19   Possible Problems

English	French	Pronunciation
...is cold	...est froid(e)	*eh frwahd*
...is too rare	...n'est pas assez cuit(e)	*neh pah zah-say kwee(t)*
...is over-cooked	...est trop cuit(e)	*tro kwee(t)*
...is tough	...est dur(e)	*eh dewr*
...is burned	...est brûlé(e)	*eh brew-lay*
...is too salty	...est trop salé(e)	*eh tro sah-lay*
...is too sweet	...est trop sucré(e)	*eh tro sew-kray*
...is too spicy	...est trop épicé(e)	*eh tro ay-pee-say*
...is spoiled	...est tourné(e)	*eh toor-nay*
...is bitter	...est aigre	*eh tehgr*
...tastes like...	...a le goût de...	*ah luh goo duh*
...is dirty	...est sale	*eh sahl*

Fancy Endings

When it's time for dessert, choose from among the
delightful specialties in Table 10.20 or from *des fromages
variés* (*day froh-mahzh vah-ryay–cheeses*): boursin, brie,
camembert, chèvre, munster, port-salut, and roquefort.
When choosing a cheese you might want to ask:

Is it...?	Est-il...?	*ch-teel*
mild	maigre	*mehgr*
sharp	piquant	*pee-kahN*
hard	ferment	*fehr-mahN-tay*
soft	à pâte molle	*ah paht mohl*

Finally, it's time for dessert, and there are so many French
specialties from which to choose. Table 10.20 will help
you make a decision.

Table 10.20   Divine Desserts

French	Pronunciation	English
une bavaroise	*ewn bah-vahr-wahz*	bavarian cream
des beignets	*day beh-nyeh*	fruit doughnuts
une bombe	*ewn bohNb*	ice cream with many flavors
une charlotte	*ewn shahr-loht*	sponge cake and pudding
une crème caramel	*ewn krehm kah-rah-mehl*	egg custard served with caramel sauce
une gaufre	*ewn gohfr*	waffle
des oeufs à la neige	*day zuh ah lah nehzh*	meringues in a custard sauce
une omelette norvégienne	*ewn nohm-leht nohr-vay-zhyehn*	baked Alaska
des poires hélène	*day pwahr ay-lehn*	poached pears with vanilla ice cream and chocolate sauce
des profiteroles	*day proh-fee-trohl*	cream puffs with chocolate sauce

Make sure you get the ice cream you want for dessert.

an ice cream	une glace	*ewn glahs*
a yogurt	un yaourt	*uhN yah-oort*
cone	un cornet	*uhN kohr-neh*
cup	une coupe	*ewn koop*
chocolate	au chocolat	*o shoh-koh-lah*
vanilla	à la vanille	*ah lah vah-nee-y*
strawberry	aux fraises	*o frehz*

Wine and Dine

The French usually drink wine with dinner. The wines you might order include the following:

red wine	le vin rouge	*luh vaN roozh*
rosé wine	le vin rosé	*luh vaN ro-zay*
white wine	le vin blanc	*luh vaN blahN*
sparkling wine	le vin mousseux	*luh vaN moo-suh*
champagne	le champagne	*luh shahN-pah-nyuh*

I Only Want a Taste

The partitive is used in French to express part of a whole, or an indefinite quantity and is equivalent to the English *some* or *any*.

Partitive	Used Before
du (de + le)	masculine singular nouns beginning with a consonant
de la	feminine singular nouns beginning with a consonant
de l'	any singular noun beginning with a vowel
des (de + les)	all plural nouns

Although *some* or *any* may be omitted in English, the partitive must always be used in French and must be repeated before each noun:

> Bring me some mousse and some coffee, please.
> Apportez-moi *de la* mousse et *du* café, s'il vous plaît.
> *ah-pohr-tay-mwah duh lah moos ay dew kah-fay seel voo pleh*

In a negative sentence, or before an adjective preceding a plural noun, the partitive is expressed by *de* (no definite article is used).

> They don't have (any) fish.
> Ils n'ont pas *de* poisson.
> *eel nohN pah duh pwah-sohN*

> He prepares good desserts.
> Il prépare de bons desserts.
> *eel pray-pahr duh bohN duh-sehr*

The Pronoun en

The pronoun *en* refers to previously mentioned things or places. *En* usually replaces *de* + noun and may mean some or any (of it/them), of it/them, about it/them, from it/them, or from there:

He wants some (of them).	I don't want any (of it).
Il veut *des pommes*.	Je ne veux pas *de viande*.
Il *en* veut.	Je n'*en* veux pas.
We speak about it.	They leave (it) from there.
Nous parlons *du café*.	Elles sortent *du restaurant*.
Nous *en* parlons.	Elles *en* sortent.

En is always expressed in French even though it may have no English equivalent or is not expressed in English:

Do you have any money?	Yes, I do.
Avez-vous *de l'argent*?	Oui, j'*en* ai.

En is placed before the verb to which its meaning is tied, usually before the conjugated verb. When there are two verbs, *en* is placed before the infinitive:

He takes (eats) some.   He wants to take (eat) some.
Il *en* prend.   Il désire *en* prendre.

Don't take (eat) any.
N'*en* prends pas.

In an affirmative command *en* changes position and is placed immediately after the verb and is joined to it by a hyphen:

Take (eat) some! (Familiar)
Prends-*en*! (*prahN zahN*)

Don't forget to ask for the check at the end of your meal:

The check please.
L'addition, s'il vous plaît.
lah-dee-syohN seel voo pleh

Chapter 11

You're a Social Butterfly

In This Chapter

➤ Amusements and diversions

➤ Invitations: extending, accepting, and refusing

You've had enough sightseeing and now you just want to relax and have some fun. You can go off to the ocean to swim and surf. Or do snow-covered mountains entice you to ski or hike? Are you a film buff or an opera lover? With the help of this chapter you'll be able to do it all and more, as well as be a guest or do the inviting.

I Love Sports!

Whether you like to relax as a beach bum, spend your days gazing out at the azure ocean, or feel compelled to engage in every fast-paced sport you can, you need certain words and terms to make your preferences known. Table 11.1 provides a list of sports and outdoor activities.

Table 11.1   Sports

One plays	On fait	*OhN feh*
aerobics	de l'aérobic (m.)	*duh lahy-roh-beek*
baseball	du base-ball	*dew bays-bohl*
basketball	du basket-ball	*dew bahs-keht bohl*
boating	du canotage	*dew kah-noh-tahzh*
cycling	du cyclisme	*dew see-kleez-muh*
fishing	de la pêche	*duh lah pehsh*
football	du football américain	*dew foot-bohl ah-may-ree-kaN*
golf	du golf	*dew gohlf*
horseback riding	de l'équitation (f.)	*duh lay-kee-tah-syohN*
hunting	de la chasse	*duh lah shahs*
jogging	du jogging	*dew zhoh-geeng*
sailing	du bateau à voiles	*dew bah-to ah vwahl*
scuba (skin) diving	de la plongée sous-marine	*duh lah plohN-zhay soo-mah-reen*
skating	du patin	*dew pah-taN*
skiing	du ski	*dew skee*
soccer	du football	*dew foot-bohl*
swimming	de la natation	*duh lah nah-tah-syohN*
tennis	du tennis	*dew teh-nees*
volleyball	du volley-ball	*dew voh-lee bohl*
waterskiing	du ski nautique	*dew skee no-teek*

Use the verb *faire* when talking about engaging in a sport.

Vous faites du tennis? (Do you play tennis?)

On fait de la pêche? (How about going fishing?)

The verbs *vouloir* (*voo-lwahr*—to want) and *pouvoir* (*poo-vwahr*—to be able to) are irregular and may be followed by the infinitive of a verb to invite someone along:

French	Pronunciation	English
je veux	*zhuh vuh*	I want
tu veux	*tew vuh*	you want
il veut	*eel vuh*	he wants
nous voulons	*noo voo-lohN*	we want
vous voulez	*voo voo-lay*	you want
ils veulent	*eel vuhl*	they want

French	Pronunciation	English
je peux	*zhuh puh*	I am able to (can)
tu peux	*tew puh*	you are able to (can)
il peut	*eel puh*	he is able to (can)
nous pouvons	*noo poo-vohN*	we are able to (can)
vous pouvez	*voo poo-vay*	you are able to (can)
ils peuvent	*eel puhv*	they are able to (can)

Vous voulez (*Tu veux*) + infinitive of a verb
Vous voulez (Tu veux) faire du patin?
Do you want to go skating?

Vous pouvez (*Tu peux*) + infinitive of a verb
Vous pouvez (Tu peux) aller à la pêche?
Can you go fishing?

An Extra Workout

Tell a friend in French which sports you like to participate in and which you prefer to watch on television. Then invite your friend along.

Other Amusement

If you're not into sports, there are plenty of other activities to keep you busy. The phrases in Table 11.2 will enable to pursue other interests. Don't forget to bring along *les jumelles* (*lay zhew-mehl*)(f.)—binoculars should you choose attend the opera, ballet, theater, or a concert.

> I would like to go…
> Je voudrais aller…
> *zhuh voo-dreh zah-lay*

Table 11.2 Places to Go

English	French	Pronunciation
to the ballet	au ballet	*o bah-leh*
to the beach	à la plage	*ah lah plahzh*
to the casino	au casino	*o kah-zee-no*
to a concert	au concert	*o kohN-sehr*
to a discotheque	à une discothèque	*ah ewn dees-koh-tehk*
to the mall	au centre commercial	*o sahNtr koh-mehr-syahl*
to the movies	au cinéma	o see-nay mah
to the opera	à l'opéra	*ah loh-pay rah*
to the theater	au théâtre	*o tay-ahtr*
to take a hike	faire une randonnée	*fehr ewn rahN-doh-nay*

At the Movies and on TV

You're all played out, you're all worked out, and your tummy is full. If you're a film buff you may want to catch the latest film or even your favorite TV program. For some quiet entertainment, ask the following questions and consult Table 11.3.

What kind of film are they showing?
On passe quel genre de film?
ohN pahs kehl zhahNr duh feelm

What's on TV?
Qu'est-ce qu'il y a à la télé?
kehs keel yah ah lah tay-lay

Table 11.3   Movies and Television Programs

English	French	Pronunciation
adventure film	un film d'aventure	*uhN feelm dah-vahN-tewr*
cartoon	un dessin animé	*uhN deh-saN ah-nee-may*
comedy	un film comique	*uhN feelm koh-meek*
game show	un jeu	*uhN zhuh*
horror movie	un film d'horreur	*uhN feelm doh-ruhr*
love story	un film d'amour	*uhN foolm dah moor*
mystery	un mystère	*uhN mees-tehr*
news	les informations (f.)	*lay zaN-fohr-mah-syohN*
police story	un film policier	*uhN feelm poh-lee-syay*
science-fiction film	un film de science-fiction	*uhN feelm duh see-ahNs-feek-syohN*
soap opera	un feuilleton (mélodramatique)	*uhN fuhy-tohN (may-loh-drah-mah-teek)*
spy movie	un film d'espionnage	*uhN feelm dehs-pee-yoh-nazh*
talk show	une causerie	*ewn koz-ree*
weather	la météo	*lay may-tay-o*

In French movie theaters, an usher, usually a young woman (une ouvreuse—*ewn noo-vruhz*) helps you select a seat to your liking and will expect a tip (un pourboire—*uhN poor-bwahr*) for services rendered. There are often at least 15 minutes of commercials shown before the main feature begins. At that time the usher comes around with a selection of candy and ice cream. Do you crave popcorn? Sorry, it's not sold! Refer to the following explanations when you choose a movie or theater:

INT-18 ans Interdit aux moins de 18 ans
Forbidden for those under 18

V.O. Version originale
Original version, subtitled

V.F. Version française
Dubbed in French

T.R. Tarif réduit
Reduced rate

C.V. Carte vermeille
"Red" senior citizens' card

Pl. Prix des places
Price of a seat

Expressing Your Opinion

If you like television, you might get hooked on *un feuilleton mélodramatique* (*uhN fuhy-tohN may-lo-drah-mah-teek*), a soap opera or any show that strikes your fancy. If you enjoy the program, you might say:

I love it!	J'adore!	*zhah-dohr*
It's a good movie.	C'est un bon film.	*seh tuhN bohN feelm*
It's amusing!	C'est amusant!	*seh tah-mew-zahN*
It's great!	C'est génial!	*seh zhay-nyahl*

| It's moving! | C'est émouvant! | *seh tay-moo-vahN* |
| It's original! | C'est original! | *seh toh-ree-zhee-nahl* |

If the show leaves something to be desired, try the following phrases:

I hate it!	Je déteste!	*zhuh day-tehst*
It's a bad movie!	C'est un mauvais film.	*seh tuhN mo-veh feelm*
It's a loser!	C'est un navet!	*seh tuhN nah-veh*
It's garbage!	C'est bidon!	*seh bee-dohN*
It's the same old thing!	C'est toujours la même chose!	*seh too-zhoor lah mehm shohz*
It's too violent!	C'est trop violent!	*sch tro vee-oh-lahN*

An Extra Workout

Look in the movie and television section of your local newspaper. Give your opinion about the movies and shows currently available.

Invitations

It isn't much fun to play alone. Why not ask someone to join you? To extend an invitation, you can ask the following:

Would you like to join me (us)?
Voudriez-vous m' (nous) accompagner?
voo-dree-yay voo mah-kohN-pah-nyay (noo zah-kohN-pah-nyay)

Whether you've been invited to play a game, to spend time at the opera, or to just visit someone at home, the following phrases will allow you to graciously accept, to cordially refuse, or to show your indifference.

Accepting

Avec plaisir.	*ah-vehk pleh-zeer*	With pleasure.
Bien entendu.	*byaN nahN-tahN-dew*	Of course.
Bien sûr.	*byaN sewr*	Of course.
C'est une bonne idée.	*seh tewn bohn ee-day*	That's a good idea.
Chouette!	*shoo-eht*	Great!
D'accord.	*dah-kohr*	O.K. (I agree)
Et comment!	*ay koh-mahN*	And how! You bet!
Il n'y a pas d'erreur.	*eel nyah pah deh-ruhr*	There's no doubt about it.
Pourquoi pas?	*poor-kwah pah*	Why not?
Si tu veux (vous voulez)	*see tew vuh (voo voo-lay)*	If you want to.
Volontiers!	*voh-lohN-tyay*	Gladly.

Refusing

C'est impossible.	*seh taN-poh-seebl*	It's impossible.
Encore!	*ahN-kohr*	Not again!
Je n'ai pas envie.	*zhuh nay pah zahN-vee*	I don't feel like it.
Je ne peux pas.	*zhuh nuh puh pah*	I can't.
Je ne suis pas libre.	*zhuh nuh swee pah leebr*	I'm not free.
Je ne veux pas.	*zhuh nuh vuh pah*	I don't want to.
Je regrette.	*zhuh ruh-greht*	I'm sorry.
Je suis désolé(e).	*zhuh swee day-zoh-lay*	I'm sorry.
Je suis fatigué(e).	*zhuh swee fah-tee-gay*	I'm tired.
Je suis occupé(e).	*zhuh swee zoh-kew-pay*	I'm busy.

Showing Indecision and Indifference

Ça dépend.	*sah day-pahN*	It depends.
Ça m'est égal.	*sah meh tay-gahl*	It's all the same to me.
Ce que tu préfères (vous préférez).	*suh kuh tew pray-fehr (voo pray-fay-ray)*	Whatever you want.
Comme tu veux (vous voulez).	*kohm tew vuh (voo voo-lay)*	Whatever you want.
Je n'ai pas de préférence.	*zhuh nay pas duh pray-fay-rahNs*	I don't have any preference.
Je ne sais pas trop.	*zhuh nuh seh pah tro*	I really don't know.
Peut-être.	*puh-tehtr*	Perhaps. Maybe.

An Extra Workout

Pick some activities from the lists in this chapter. Imagine that you have to respond to an invitation to participate in them. Practice giving your answers in French.

Chapter 12

Personal Services

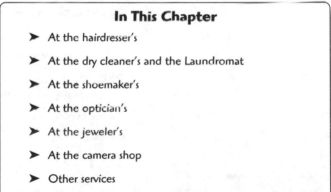

In This Chapter

➤ At the hairdresser's

➤ At the dry cleaner's and the Laundromat

➤ At the shoemaker's

➤ At the optician's

➤ At the jeweler's

➤ At the camera shop

➤ Other services

Good grief! Your roots are showing! You've spilled some ketchup on your new white shorts! Your left contact lens just ripped! Your toddler decided to play with your watch in the bathtub! What should you do? Don't worry. It's not a catastrophe. Just consult the concierge of your hotel or consult *les pages jaunes* (*lay pahzh zhon*), the yellow pages. Everything will work out in the end.

A Very Bad Hair Day!

Today's new unisex establishments have put an end to past tradition where men went *chez le coiffeur* (to the barber's) and women went *au salon de beauté* (to the beauty parlor). More and more, men and women are demanding similar services. To get what you want simply ask:

Could you give me...	I would like...
Pourriez-vous me donner...	Je voudrais...
poo-ryay voo muh doh-nay	*zhuh voo-dreh*

Today's salons provide the services listed in Table 12.1.

Table 12.1 At the Salon

English	French	Pronunciation
a facial	un massage facial	*uhN mah-sahzh fah-syahl*
a haircut	une coupe de cheveux	*ewn koop duh shuh-vuh*
a manicure	une manucure	*ewn mah-new-kewr*
a pedicure	une pédicurie	*ewn pay-dee-kew-ree*
a permanent	une permanente	*ewn pehr-mah-nahNt*
a rinse	un rinçage colorant	*uhN raN-sahzh koh-loh-rahN*
a set	une mise en plis	*ewn mee-zohN plee*
a shampoo	un shampooing	*uhN shahN-pwaN*
a trim	une coupe	*ewn koop*
a waxing	une épilation	*ewn ay-pee-lah-syohN*
highlights	des reflets	*day ruh-fleh*
layers	une coupe dégradée	*ewn koop day-grah-day*

Do you need other services? Table 12.2 provides the phrases you need to get them. Use the following phrase to preface your request:

Could you please…?
Pourriez-vous…s'il vous plaît?
poo-ryay voo…seel voo pleh

Table 12.2 Other Services

English	French	Pronunciation
blow dry my hair	me donner un brushing	*muh doh-nay uhN bruh-sheeng*
curl my hair	me friser les cheveux	*muh free-zay lay shuh vuh*
shave my beard (mustache)	me raser la barbe (la moustache)	*muh rah-zay lah bahrb (lah moo-stahsh)*
straighten my hair	me défriser les cheveux	*muh day-free-zay lay shuh-vuh*
trim my bangs	me rafraîchir la frange	*muh rah-freh-sheer lah frahNzh*
trim my beard (mustache, sideburns)	me rafraîchir la barbe (la moustache, les pattes)	*muh rah-freh-sheer lah bahrb (lah moo-stahsh, lay paht)*

Getting What You Want

When there's a language barrier, there's no end to the disasters that could befall you, as you try to get the cut, style, and color you desire. The following phrases will help you make yourself perfectly clear:

I prefer my hair…
Je préfère mes cheveux…
zhuh pray-fehr may vuh

I'd like a… style…
Je voudrais une coiffure…
zhuh voo-dreh zewn kwah-shuh-fewr

English	French	Pronunciation
long	longs	*lohN*
medium	mi-longs	*mee-lohN*

continues

continued

English	French	Pronunciation
short	courts	*koor*
wavy	frisés	*free-zay*
curly	bouclés	*boo-klay*
straight	raides (lissés)	*rehd (lee-say)*

Does your hair sometimes feel stiff and gooey after a stylist has coated it with mousse, gel, or spray? How do you feel about all those chemicals seeping into your skull? Are you allergic to certain products? If you don't want something on your hair, don't be afraid to tell the hairdresser.

> Don't put on any...please.
> Ne mettez pas de (d')...s'il vous plaît.
> *nuh meh-tay pah duh...seel voo pleh*

English	French	Pronunciation
conditioner	après-shampooing	*ah-preh shahN-pwaN*
gel	gel coiffant (m.)	*zhehl kwah-fahN*
hairspray	laque (f.)	*lahk*
mousse	mousse coiffante (f.)	*moos kwah-fahN*
shampoo	shampooing (m.)	*shahN-pwaN*

Don't forget to ask about tipping:

> Is the tip included?
> Le service est compris?
> *luh sehr-vees eh kohN-pree*

Problems in General

Some handy, key phrases will help you in most situations.
Keep them on hand whether you go to the dry cleaner, the
shoemaker, the optometrist, the jeweler, or the camera store.

At what time do you open (close)?
Vous êtes ouvert (vous fermez) à quelle heure?
voo zeh too-vehr (voo fehr-may) ah kehl uhr

What days are you open? Closed?
Vous êtes ouvert (vous fermez) quels jours?
voo zeht oo-vehr (voo fehr-may) kehl zhoor

Can you fix...for me?
Pouvez-vous me réparer...?
poo-vay voo muh ray-pah-ray

Can you fix it (them) today?
Pouvez-vous le (la, l', les) réparer aujourd'hui?
poo-vay voo luh (lah, lay) ray-pah-ray o-zhoor-dwee

May I have a receipt?
Puis-je avoir un reçu?
pweezh ah-vwahr uhN ruh-sew

Can you fix it (them) temporarily (while I wait)?
Pouvez-vous le (la, l', les) réparer provisoirement
(pendant que j'attends)?
*poo-vay voo luh (lah, lay) ray-pah-ray proh-vee-zwahr-
mahN (pahN-dahN kuh zhah-tahN)*

How much do I owe you?
Je vous dois combien?
zhuh voo dwah kohN-byaN

At the Dry Cleaner's—à la Teinturerie

I don't like that rumpled look—like I slept in my clothes
for a week. I'm embarrassed by ugly stains that I've over-
looked—you know, those yellow ones that always seem to

crop up on white clothes. Don't despair. If you know how to express yourself, your stains, spots, tears, and wrinkles will be history.

I have a problem.
J'ai un problème.
zhay uhN proh-blehm

What's the problem?
Quel est le problème?
kehl eh luh proh-blehm

There is (are)...
Il y a...
eel yah

English	French	Pronunciation
a hole	un trou	*uhN troo*
a missing button	un bouton qui manque	*uhN boo-tohN kee mahNk*
a spot	une tache	*ewn tahsh*
a tear	une déchirure	*ewn day-shee-rewr*

Once the problem has been explained, state what you'd like done about it:

Can you (dry) clean this (these)...for me?
Vous pouvez me nettoyer (à sec) ce (cette, cet, ces)...?
voo poo-vay muh neh-twah-yay ah sehk suh (seht, seht, say)

Can you please mend this (these)...for me?
Vous pouvez me faire recoudre ce (cette, cet, ces)...?
voo poo-vay muh fehr ruh-koodr suh (seht, seht, say)

Can you please press this (these)...for me?
Vous pouvez me repasser (réparer) ce (cette, cet, ces)...?
voo poo-vay muh ruh-pah-say (ray-pah-ray) suh (seht, seht, say)

Can you please starch this (these)...for me?
Vous pouvez m'amidonner ce (cette, cet, ces)...?
voo poo-vay mah-mee-doh-nay suh (seht, seht, say)

I need it (them)...
J'en ai besoin...
zhahN nay buh-zwaN

English	French	Pronunciation
today	aujourd'hui	*o-zhoord-wee*
this afternoon	cet après-midi	*seht ah-preh mee-dee*
tonight	ce soir	*suh swahr*
tomorrow	demain	*duh-maN*
the day after tomorrow	après-demain	*ah-preh duh-maN*
next week	la semaine prochaine	*lah suh-mehn proh-shehn*

At the Laundromat—à la Blanchisserie or à la Laverie Automatique

Laundry piles up quickly when you're on vacation. If it can't wait till you get home, a trip to a Laundromat could save you a bundle. Use the following phrases to get the information you need.

I'd like to wash my clothes.
Je voudrais laver mes vêtements.
zhuh voo-dreh lah-vay may veht-mahN

I'd like to have my clothes washed.
Je voudrais faire laver mes vêtements.
zhuh voo-dreh fehr lah-vay may veht-mahN

Are you mortified by that ring around your collar? Or perhaps you're afraid that your beautiful new silk skirt will get ruined by an amateur. If you're intent on doing the job yourself, use the following phrases:

Is there a free washing machine (dryer)?
Y a-t-il une machine à laver (un séchoir) libre?
ee ah-tee ewn mah-sheen ah lah-vay (uhN saysh-wahr) leebr

Where can I buy soap powder?
Où puis-je acheter de la lessive en poudre?
oo pweezh ahsh-tay duh lah leh-seev ahN poodr

At the Shoemaker's—Chez le Cordonnier

Your shoelace broke, you've worn a hole in the sole of your shoe from walking so much, or you just need a good shine. Use the following phrases to help you.

Can you repair...for me?
Pouvez-vous me réparer...?
poo-vay voo muh ray-pah-ray

English	French	Pronunciation
these shoes	ces chaussures	*say sho-sewr*
these boots	ces bottes	*say boht*
this heel	ce talon	*suh tah-lohN*
this sole	cette semelle	*seht suh-mehl*

Do you sell shoelaces?
Vendez-vous des lacets?
vahN-day-voo day lah-seh

I'd like a shoe shine.
Je voudrais un cirage.
zhuh voo-dreh zuhN see-rage

When can I have them?
Quand puis-je les avoir?
kahN pweezh lay zah-vwahr

I need them by Friday (without fail).
Il me les faut vendredi (sans faute, assurément).
eel muh lay fo vahN-druh-dee (sahN fot, ah-sew-ray-mahN)

At the Optometrist's—Chez l'Opticien

For those who are visually challenged, losing or tearing a pair of contacts, or breaking a frame or lens of a pair of glasses could prove a disaster. If you depend on optical necessities, familiarize yourself with the following phrases:

Can you repair these glasses for me?
Pouvez-vous me réparer ces lunettes?
poo-vay voo muh ray-pah-ray say lew-neht

The lens (the frame) is broken.
Le verre (la monture) est cassé(e).
Luh vehr (lah mohN-tewr) eh kah-say

Can you tighten the screws?
Pouvez-vous resserrer les vis?
poo-vay voo ruh-seh-ray lay vees

Can you replace this contact lens?
Pouvez-vous remplacer cette lentille (ce verre) de contact?
poo-vay voo rahN-plah-say seht lahN-tee-y (suh vehr) duh kohN-tahkt

I need the glasses (contacts) as soon as possible.
Il me faut les lunettes (les verres de contact) aussitôt que possible.
eel muh fo lay lew-neht (luy vehr duh kohN-tahkt) o-see-to kuh poh-seebl

Can you fix them quickly?
Pouvez-vous les réparer vite?
poo-vay voo lay ray-pah-ray veet

Do you sell sunglasses?
Vendez-vous des lunettes de soleil?
vahN-day voo day lew-neht duh soh-lehy

At the Jeweler's—Chez le Bijoutier

What luck! Your watch has gone haywire in the middle of your trip. Use the following phrases if you need it repaired before returning home:

Can you repair this watch?
Pouvez-vous réparer cette montre?
poo-vay voo ray-pah-ray seht mohNtr

My watch doesn't work.
Ma montre ne marche pas.
mah mohNtr nuh mahrsh pah

My watch is fast (slow).	Do you sell bands
Ma montre avance	(batteries)?
(retarde).	Vendez-vous des bandes
ma mohNtr ah-vahNs	(des piles)?
(ruh-tahrd)	*vahN-day voo day*
	bahnd (day peel)

My watch has stopped.	When will it be ready?
Ma montre s'est arrêtée	Quand sera-t-elle prête?
mah mohNtr seh tah-reh-tay	*kahN suh-rah tehl preht*

At the Camera Shop—au Magasin de Photographie

When we're on a fabulous vacation, it's very important to most of us to capture on film those special moments and unforgettable landscapes. If you need to visit a camera shop or film store in a French speaking country, the following words and phrases will come in handy.

a camera	un appareil-photo	*uhN nah-pah-rahy foh-to*
a video camera	un appareil vidéo	*uhN nah-pah-rahy vee-day-o*

If you have special needs, you might ask:

Can you fix this camera?
Pouvez-vous réparer cet appareil-photo?
poo-vay voo ray-pah-ray seht ah-pah-rehy-foh-to

The film doesn't advance.	I need a new battery.
Le film n'avance pas.	Il me faut une nouvelle
luh feelm nah-vahns pah	pile.
	eel muh fo tewn noo-vehl
	peel

How much will the repair cost?
Combien coûtera la réparation?
kohN-byaN koot-rah lah ray-pah-rah-syohN

I need it as soon as possible.
J'en ai besoin aussitôt que possible.
zhaN nay buh-zwaN o-see-to kuh poh-seebl

Do you sell rolls of 20 (36) exposure film in color (black
and white)?
Vendez-vous des pellicules de vingt (trente-six) en
couleur (noir et blanc)?
*vahN-day voo day peh-lee-kewl duh vaN (trahNt-sees) ahN
koo-luhr (nwahr ay blahN)*

Other Services

You might also need special services from time to time.
You might, for example, need to find your consulate to
report a lost passport. Or perhaps your wallet has been
stolen and you'd like to file a police report. You might
even want a translator to help you when you're too upset
to speak a foreign language. The following phrases should
help:

Where is...
Où est...
oo eh

the police station?
le commissariat de police?
luh koh-mee-sah-ryah duh poh-lees

the American consulate?
le consulat américain?
luh kohN-sew-lah ah-may-ree-kaN

the American embassy?
l'ambassade américaine?
lahN-bah-sahd ah-may-ree-kehn

I lost...
J'ai perdu...
zhay pehr-dew

> my passport.
> mon passeport.
> *mohN pahs-pohr*

> my wallet.
> mon portefeuille.
> *mohN pohr-tuh-fuhy*

Help me, please.
Aidez-moi, s'il vous plaît.
eh-day mwah seel voo pleh

I need an interpreter.
Il me faut un interprète.
eel muh fo tuhN naN-tehr-preht

Does anyone here speak English?
Y a-t-il quelqu'un qui parle anglais?
ee ah teel kehl kuhN kee pahrl ahN-gleh

An Extra Workout

Pretend you are having a problem in a French-speaking country. Explain what the matter is in French and get help.

Chapter 13

There's a Doctor on Call

In This Chapter

➤ All about your body

➤ Signs, symptoms, and illnesses

➤ Saying how long you've felt this way

➤ Reflexive verbs

➤ At the pharmacy

Invariably at the worst possible moment, people get sick or have accidents. The situation can become difficult, if not critical when you can't communicate the problem. In this chapter, you will learn how to explain your ailments and how long you've been experiencing the symptoms.

Does It Hurt Here or There?

When traveling, it pays to be prepared in case illness strikes. Start by familiarizing yourself with the parts of the body in Table 13.1.

Table 13.1 Parts of the Body

English	French	English	French
arm	le bras (*luh brah*)	back	le dos (*luh do*)
chest	la poitrine (*lah pwah-treen*)	ear	l'oreille (f.) (*loh-rehy*)
elbow	le coude (*luh kood*)	eye	l'oeil (m.) (*luhy*)
eyes	les yeux (*lay zyuh*)	face	la figure, le visage (*lah fee-gewr, luh vee-zahzh*)
finger	le doigt (*luh dwah*)	foot	le pied (*luh pyay*)
hand	la main (*lah maN*)	head	la tête (*lah teht*)
heart	le coeur (*luh kuhr*)	hip	la hanche (*lah ahNsh*)
kidney	le rein (*luh raN*)	knee	le genou (*luh zhuh-noo*)
leg	la jambe (*lah zhahNb*)	lip	la lèvre (*lah lehvr*)
lung	le poumon (*luh poo-mohN*)	mouth	la bouche (*lah boosh*)
neck	le cou (*luh koo*)	nose	le nez (*luh nay*)
shoulder	l'épaule (*lay-pohl*)	stomach	l'estomac (m.) (*leh-stoh-mah*)
throat	la gorge (*lah gohrzh*)	toe	l'orteil (m.) (*lohr-tehy*)
tongue	la langue (*lah lahNg*)	tooth	la dent (*lah dahN*)
wrist	le poignet (*luh pwah-nyeh*)		

If you run into a problem and have to seek medical attention, the obvious first question will be: "What's the matter with you?," "Qu'est-ce que vous avez?" (*kehs kuh voo zah-vay*). To say what hurts or bothers you, use the expression *avoir mal à* + definite article:

Do you have a stomach ache?
Tu as mal à l'estomac?
tew ah ah lehs-toh-mah

Our feet hurt.
Nous avons mal aux pieds.
noo zah-vohN mahl opyay

Full Speed Ahead

If you have to go to the dentist, use the expression *avoir mal aux dents* (to have a toothache) or *avoir une rage de dents* (to have a very bad toothache).

I've got a toothache.	He has a very bad toothache.
Elle a mal aux dents.	Il a une rage de dents.

What Are Your Symptoms?

If you need to provide a more detailed description of your aches and pains use the symptoms and conditions listed in Table 13.2. Use the phrase *J'ai (zhay)*—I have—to preface your complaint.

Table 13.2   Symptoms

English	French	Pronunciation
bruise	une contusion	*ewn kohN-tew-zyohN*
bump	une bosse	*ewn bohs*
burn	une brûlure	*ewn brew-lewr*
chills	des frissons	*day free-sohN*
cough	une toux	*ewn too*
cramps	des crampes	*day krahNp*
cut	une coupure	*ewn koo-pewr*
diarrhea	de la diarrhée	*dun lah dee-ah-ray*
fever	de la fièvre	*duh lah fyehvr*
fracture	une fracture	*ewn frahk-tewr*
lump	une grosseur	*ewn groh-sewr*

continues

Table 13.2 Continued

English	French	Pronunciation
pain	une douleur	*ewn doo-luhr*
rash	une éruption	*ewn nay-rewp-syohN*
sprain	une foulure	*ewn foo-lewr*
swelling	une enflure	*ewn nahN-flewr*
wound	une blessure	*ewn bleh-sewr*

Here are some other phrases that might prove useful when explaining how you're feeling:

I'm coughing.
Je tousse.
zhuh toos

I'm sneezing.
J'éternue.
zay-tehr-new

I'm bleeding.
Je saigne.
zhuh seh-nyuh

I'm constipated.
Je suis constipé(e).
zhuh swee kohN-stee-pay

I'm nauseous.
J'ai des nausées.
zhay day no-zay

I have trouble sleeping.
J'ai du mal à dormir.
zhay dew mahl ah dohr-meer

I feel bad.
Je me sens mal.
zhuh muh sahN mahl

I hurt everywhere.
J'ai mal partout.
zhay mahl pahr-too

I feel weak.
Je me sens faible.
zhuh muh sahN fehbl

I'm dizzy.
J'ai le vertige.
zhay luh vehr-teezh

The Doctor Wants to Know

You might have to answer many personal questions about your general health and family history so the doctor can treat you properly. Refer to Table 13.3 for the words you'll need.

Have you had…?	Do you suffer from…?
Avez-vous subi (eu)…?	Souffrez-vous de (d')…?
ah-vay voo sew-bee(ew)	*soo-fray voo duh*

Table 13.3   Other Symptoms and Illness

English	French	Pronunciation
allergic reaction	une réaction allergique	*ewn ray-ahk-syohN ah-lehr-zheek*
angina	une angine	*ewn nahN-zheen*
appendicitis	l'appendicite (f.)	*lah-pahN-dee-seet*
asthma	l'asthme (m.)	*lahz-muh*
bronchitis	la bronchite	*lah brohN-sheet*
cancer	le cancer	*luh kahN-sehr*
diabetes	le diabète	*luh dee-ah-beht*
dizziness	le vertige	*luh vehr-teezh*
hay fever	le rhume des foins	*luh rewm day fwaN*
heart attack	une crise cardiaque	*ewn kreez kahr-dyahk*
hepatitis	l'hépatite	*lay-pah-teet*
pneumonia	la pneumonie	*lah pnuh-moh-nee*
stroke	une attaque d'apoplexie	*ewn nah-tahk dah-poh-plehk-see*
tuberculosis	la tuberculose	*lah tew-behr-kew-lohz*

Remember to give the doctor any pertinent information that might help him/her serve you better. You might need some of the following phrases:

I've had this pain since…
J'ai cette douleur depuis…
zhay seht doo-luhr duh-pwee

There's a (no) family history of…
Il (n') y a (pas) de fréquence de…
eel (nyah) yah (pah) duh fray-kahNs duh

I am (not) allergic to...
Je (ne) suis (pas) allérgique à...
zhuh (nuh) swee (pah) (zah-lehr-geek) âh

I had... ...years ago.
J'ai subi...il y a...ans.
zhay sew-bee...eel yah...ahN

I'm taking...	I'm pregnant.
Je prends...	Je suis enceinte.
zhuh prahN	*zhuh swee zahN-saNt*

Want to know how serious it is? Ask the following:

Is it serious?	Is it contagious?
C'est grave?	C'est contagieux?
seh grahv	*seh kohN-tah-zhyuh*

How often do I take this medicine?
Combien de fois par jour faut-il prendre ce
médicament?
*kohN-byaN duh fwah pahr zhoor fo-teel prahNdr suh
may-dee-kah-mahN*

How long do I have to stay in bed?
Combien de temps dois-je garder le lit?
kohN-byaN duh tahN dwahzh gahr-day luh lee

May I please have a receipt for my medical insurance?
Puis-je avoir une quittance pour mon assurance
maladie?
*pweezh ah-vwahr ewn kee-tahNs poor mohN nah-sew
rahNs mah-lah-dee*

How Long Has This Been Going On?

Doctors always ask how long you've been experiencing
your symptoms. This information is extremely important
for a correct diagnosis. The phrases in Table 13.4 suggest
the number of ways you may hear the question posed and
the ways in which to answer the question.

Table 13.4 How Long Have Your Symptoms Lasted?

Question	Answer
Since when... Depuis quand... (*duh-pwee kahN*)	Since... Depuis... (*duh-pwee*)
How long has (have)...been... Depuis combien de temps... (*duh-pwee kohN-byaN duh tahN*)	For... Depuis... (*duh-pwee*)
How long has...(have)...been... Combien de temps y a-t-il que... (*kohN-byaN duh than ee ah-teel kuh*)	For... Il y a + time + que... (*eel yah + time + kuh*)
How long has (have)...been... Ça fait combien de temps que... (*sah feh kohN-byaN duh tahN kuh*)	For... Ça fait + time + que... (*sah feh + time + kuh*), Voilà + time + que (*vwah-lah + time + que*)
How long have you been suffering? Depuis combien de temps souffrez-vous? (*duh-pwee kohN-byaN duh tahN soo-fray voo*)	For three days. Depuis trois jours. (*duh-pwee trwah zhoor*)
Since when have you been suffering? Depuis quand souffrez-vous? (*duh-pwee kahN soo-fray voo*)	Since yesterday. Depuis hier. (*duh-pwee yehr*)
How long have you been suffering? Combien de temps y a-t-il que vous souffrez? (*kohN-byaN duh tahN ee ah-teel kuh voo soo-fray*)	For two days. Il y a deux jours. (*eel yah duh zhoor*)
How long have you been suffering? Ça fait combien de temps que vous souffrez? (*sah feh kohN-byaN duh tahN kuh voo soo-fray*)	It's been a week./ For a week. Ça fait une semaine./ Voilà une semaine. (*sah feh tewn suh-mehn/ vwah-lah ewn suh-mehn*)

An Extra Workout

Practice having an imaginary conversation with a doctor.
Describe how you feel, your symptoms, and how long
you've felt this way.

Reflexive Verbs

A reflexive pronoun shows that the subject is performing
an action upon itself. The subject and the reflexive pronoun refer to the same person(s) or thing(s): *She* hurt *her-
self*. *They* enjoy *themselves*.

Use the following pronouns when the verb is reflexive.
Put these pronouns in the same position as direct and
indirect object pronouns, *y* and *en*:

me (myself)	nous (ourselves)
te (yourself)	vous (yourself[selves])
se (him/herself)	se (themselves)

Full Speed Ahead

Reflexive verbs can always be identified by the *se* that
precedes the infinitive.

At the Pharmacy

In general, when traveling outside the United States, you should not expect to find a pharmacy that carries the wide range of supplies found in many of our drug stores: stationery, cards, cosmetics, candy, and household items. In France, *a pharmacie* is easily identified by a green cross above the door. It sells prescription drugs, over-the-counter medications, items intended for personal hygiene, and some cosmetics. If the pharmacy is closed, look for a sign on the door telling customers where they can locate a neighboring pharmacy that is open all night *(une pharmacie de garde)*.

A *droguerie* sells chemical products, paints, household cleansers and accessories (mops, brooms, buckets), and some hygiene and beauty products, but does not dispense prescriptions.

A *drugstore* is like a small department store; it stocks personal hygiene items, books, magazines, newspapers, records, maps, guides, gifts and souvenirs, but no prescription medicine. Additionally, you may also find fast-food restaurants, a bar, and even a movie theater.

If you are indeed trying to find the closest drugstore, you might want to ask:

Where's the nearest pharmacy?
Où est la pharmacie la plus proche.
oo eh lah fahr-mah-see lah plew prohsh

When you speak to the druggist, you would say:

Could you please fill this prescription (immediately)?
Pourriez-vous exécuter (tout de suite) cette ordonnance, s'il vous plaît?
poo-ryay voo ehg-zay-kew-tay (toot sweet) seht ohr-doh-nahNs seel voo pleh

How long will it take?
Ça prendra combien de temps?
sah prahN-drah kohN-byaN duh tahN

For your over the counter needs, consult Table 13.5 will help you find it. Begin by saying to a clerk: *Je cherche...* (*zhuh shersh*)—I'm looking for...

Table 13.5   Drugstore Items

English	French	Pronunciation
alcohol	de l'alcool	*duh lahl-kohl*
antacid	un anti-acide	*uhN nahN-tee ah-seed*
antihistamine	un antihistaminique	*uhN nahn-tee-ees-tah-mee-neek*
antiseptic	un antiseptique	*uhN nahN-tee-sehp-teek*
aspirins	des aspirines	*day zah-spee-reen*
bandages (wound)	des pansements (m.)	*day pahNs-mahN*
Band-aid	un pansement adhésif	*uhn pahNs-mahN ahd-ay-zeef*
bobby pins	des épingles à cheveux (f.)	*day zay-paNgl ah shuh-vuh*
bottle	un biberon	*uhN beeb-rohN*
brush	une brosse	*ewn brohs*
cleansing cream	une crème démaquillante	*ewn krehm day-mah-kee-yahNt*
comb	un peigne	*uhN peh-nyuh*
condoms	des préservatifs (m.)	*day pray-zehr-vah-teef*
cotton (absorbent)	du coton de l'ouate	*dew koh-tohN duh lwaht*
cough drops	des pastilles (f.)	*day pah-stee-y*
cough syrup	le sirop contre la toux	*luh see-roh kohNtr lah too*
deodorant	du déodorant	*dew day-oh-doh-rahN*
diapers (disposable)	des couches (disponibles) (m.)	*day koosh dees-poh-neebl*

English	French	Pronunciation
emery boards	des limes à ongles	*day leem ah ohNgl*
eye drops	les gouttes pour les yeux, du collyre	*lay goot poor lay zyuh, dew koh-leer*
gauze pads	des bandes de gaze (f.)	*day bahnd duh gahz*
heating pad	un thermoplasme	*uhN tehr-moh-plahz-muh*
ice pack	une vessie de glace	*ewn veh-see duh glahs*
laxative (mild)	un laxatif (léger)	*uhN lahk-sah-teef (lay-zhay)*
makeup	du maquillage	*dew mah-kee-yahzh*
mouthwash	un dentifrice	*uhN dahN-tee-frees*
nail clippers	un coupe-ongles	*uhN koop ohNgl*
nail file	une lime à ongles	*ewn leem ah ohNgl*
nail polish remover	du dissolvant	*dew dee-sohl-vahn*
nose drops	des gouttes nasales (f.)	*day goot nah-zahl*
pacifier	une sucette	*ewn sew-seht*
razor (electric)	un rasoir (électrique)	*uhN rah-zwahr (ay-lehk-treek)*
razor blades	des lames de rasoir (f.)	*day lahm duh rah-zwahr*
safety pins	des épingles de sûreté (f.)	*day zay-paNgl duh sewr-tay*
sanitary napkins	des serviettes hygiéniques (f.)	*day sehr-vyeht ee-zhyay-nek*
shampoo anti-dandruff	du shampooing anti-pellicules	*dew shahN-pwaN ahN-tee peh-lee-kewl*
shaving cream	de la crème à raser	*duh lah krehm ah rah-zay*
sleeping pills	des somnifères (m.)	*day sohm-nee-fehr*
soap (bar)	une savonette	*ewn sah-voh-neht*
suntan lotion	de la lotion solaire	*duh lah loh-syohN soh-lehr*
talcum powder	du talc	*dew tahlk*
tampons	des tampons périodiques (m.)	*day tahN-pohN pay-ree-oh-deek*

continues

Table 13.5   Continued

English	French	Pronunciation
thermometer	un thermomètre	*uhN tehr-mo-mehtr*
tissues	des mouchoirs en papier (m.)	*day moosh-wahr ahN pah-pyay*
toothbrush	une brosse à dents	*ewn brohs ah dahN*
toothpaste	de la pâte dentifrice	*duh lah paht dahN-tee-frees*
tweezers	une pince à épiler	*ewn paNs ah ay-pee-lay*
vitamins	des vitamines (f.)	*day vee-tah-meen*

Special Items

For information or the rental of items for the physically challenged, listed in Table 13.6, go to a pharmacy that specializes in *la location d'appareils médiaux* (*lah loh-kah-syohn dah-pah-rehy may-dee-yo*).

> Where can I get...?
> Où puis-je obtenir...?
> *oo pweezh ohb-tuh-neer*

Table 13.6   Special Needs

English	French	Pronunciation
cane	une canne	*ewn kahn*
crutches	des béquilles	*day bay-kee*
walker	un déambulateur	*uhN day-ahN-bew-lah-tuhr*
wheelchair	un fauteuil roulant	*uhN fo-tuhy roo-lahN*

An Extra Workout

Put French labels on the drugstore items you keep in stock. Every time you open the door to your medicine cabinet, memorize the name of at least two items you frequently use.

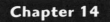

Chapter 14

Taking Care of Business

In This Chapter

➤ How to make a phone call

➤ Dealing with your mail

➤ Faxes, photocopies, and computers

Conducting business in a foreign country is always a bit of a challenge. It's crucial to understand how to place a phone call, send a letter, buy necessary stationery supplies, and deal with faxes and photocopies. Being computer literate in any language is probably one of the most important skills you'll need to possess. This chapter will help you deal with it all.

Phone Calls

If you plan to call long distance from a foreign country, whether for business or for pleasure, expect that someone will have to explain how to use the local phone system.

It is also quite probable that the procedures for making local calls will be different from what you are accustomed to back home. You will want to make sure to correctly express the type of call you want to make. Table 14.1 provides you with some options.

Table 14.1   Types of Phone Calls

English	French	Pronunciation
collect call	la communication en P.C.V.	*lah koh-mew-nee-kah-syohN ahN pay-say-vay*
credit-card call	la communication par carte de crédit	*lah koh-mew-nee-kah-syohN pahr kahrt duh kray-dee*
local call	la communication locale	*lah koh-mew-nee-kah-syohN loh-kahl*
long-distance call	la communication interurbaine	*lah koh-mew-nee-kah-syohN aN-tehr-ewr-behn*
out of the country call	la communication à l'étranger	*lah koh-mew-nee-kah-syohN ah lay-trahN-zhay*
person-to-person call	la communication avec préavis	*lah koh-mew-nee-kah-syohN ah-vehk pray-ah-vee*

Full Speed Ahead

Public pay phones are located in some post offices, cafés and stores, and are on the streets of larger cities. Many of these phones provide calling instructions in several languages.

Table 14.2 provides the words to help you understand French directions for placing a phone call.

Table 14.2   How to Make a Phone Call

English	French	Pronunciation
to call	téléphoner, appeler	*tay-lay-foh-nay, rah-play*
to call back	rappeler, retéléphoner	*rah-play, ruh-tay-lay-fohn-nay*
to dial	composer (faire) le numéro	*kohN-po-zay (fehr) luh new-may-ro*
to hang up (the receiver)	raccrocher, quitter	*rah-kroh-shay (kee-tay)*
to insert the card	introduire la carte	*aN-troh-dweer lah kahrt*
to know the area code	savoir l'indicatif, du pays (country), de la ville (city)	*sah-vwahr laN-dee-kah-teef, dew pay-ee, duh lah veel*
to leave a message	laisser un message	*leh-say uhN meh-sahzh*
to listen for the dial tone	attendre la tonalité	*ah-tahNdr lah toh-nah-lee-tay*
to pick up (the receiver)	décrocher	*day-kroh-shay*
to telephone	téléphoner, appeler par téléphone, donner un coup de fil	*tay-lay-foh-nay, ah-play pahr tay-lay-fohn, doh-nay uhN koo duh feel*

Phone Talk

Understanding telephone replies in a foreign language is far more difficult than face-to-face conversations, because you're not able to observe a person's body language. Additionally, telephones tend to distort voices and sounds. It would be wise for you to familiarize yourself with the expressions used when making and answering a phone call. Table 14.3 will show you how to begin a telephone conversation.

Table 14.3   Making a Phone Call

Calling	Answering
hello allô (*ah-lo*)	hello allô (*ah-lo*)
Is this the...residence? Je suis bien chez...? (*zhuh swee byaN shay*)	Who's calling? Qui est à l'appareil? (*kee eh tah lah-pah-rehy*)
It's... C'est... (*seh*)	This is... Ici... (*ee-see*)
Is... in (*there*)? ...est là? (*eh lah*)	Hold on/Just a moment Un moment/Il (Elle) n'est pas là (*uhN moh-mahN*)/(*eel [ehl] neh pah lah*)
I would like to speak to... Je voudrais parler à... (*zhuh voo-dreh pahr-lay ah*)	He (She) is not in. Ne quittez (quitte) pas. (*nuh kee-tay (keet) pah*)
When will he(she) be back? Quand sera-t-il (elle) de retour? (*kahN suh-rah-teel [tehl] duh ruh-toor*)	Do you want to leave a message? Voulez-vous (veux-tu) laisser un message? (*voo-lay voo [vuh-tew] leh-say uhN meh-sahzh*)
I'll call back later. Je vais rappeler plus tard. (*zhuh veh rah-play plew tahr*)	

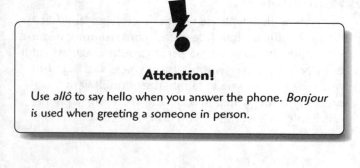

Attention!

Use *allô* to say hello when you answer the phone. *Bonjour* is used when greeting a someone in person.

Problems

Are you having trouble reaching your party? The following are some phrases you might say or hear when you are
having problems:

What number are you calling?
Vous demandez quel numéro?
voo duh-mahN-day kehl new-may-ro

It's a mistake.	(I have) You have the
C'est une erreur.	wrong number.
seh tewn eh-ruhr	(J'ai) Vous avez le mauvais
	numéro.
	(zhay) voo zah-vay luh
	moh-veh new-may-ro

What's the problem?	We got cut off
Quel en est le problème?	(disconnected).
kehl ahN eh luh proh-blehm	On nous a coupés.
	ohN noo zah koo-pay

Please redial the number.
Recomposez le numéro, s'il vous plaît.
ruh-kohN-poh-zay luh new-may-ro seel voo pleh

The telephone is out of order.
Le téléphone est en panne (hors de service).
luh tay-lay-fohn eh tahN pahn (tohr dsehr-vees)

There's a lot of static on the line.
Il y a beaucoup de parasites sur la ligne.
eel yah bo-koo duh pah-rah-seet sewr lah lee-nyuh

I'll Write, Instead

It's far more cost effective to send a letter than to place a
long-distance call. Table 14.4 provides the vocabulary you
need to send your mail.

Table 14.4   Mail and Post Office Terms

English	French	Pronunciation
address	l'addresse (f.)	*lah-drehs*
addressee	le destinataire	*luh dehs-tee-nah-tehr*
air letter	l'aérogramme (m.)	*lahy-roh-grahm*
envelope	l'enveloppe (f.)	*lahN-vlohp*
letter	la lettre	*lah lehtr*
mailbox	la boîte aux lettres	*lah bwaht o lehtr*
money order	le mandat-poste	*luh mahN-dah pohst*
package	le paquet	*luh pah-keh*
postcard	la carte postale	*lah kahrt pohs-tahl*
postage	l'affranchissement (m.)	*lah-frahN-shees-mahN*
postal code	le code postal (régional)	*luh kohd pohs-tahl (ray-zhoh-nahl)*
rate	le tarif	*luh tah-reef*
sheet of stamps	la feuille de timbres	*lah fuhy duh taNbr*
stamp	le timbre	*luh taNbr*

In France, many post offices open as early as 8 a.m., close as late as 7 p.m., and may take a two hour lunch break! There is a main branch in Paris which is always open. Stamps may be purchased at some cafés, bureaux de tabac, and hotels. If you don't want to take a trip to the post office, look for a yellow mailbox.

Getting Service

You've written all the letters and post cards you felt obligated to write and now you're ready to send them off. If you don't know where a post office or mailbox is located, simply ask:

Where is the nearest post office (mailbox)?
Où se trouve (est) le bureau de poste le plus proche
(la boîte aux lettres la plus proche)?
oo suh troov (eh) luh bew-ro duh pohst luh plew prohsh
(lah bwaht o lehtr lah plew prohsh)

Depending upon the type of letters and packages you wish
to send, special forms, paperwork, postage rates are necessary. It is important to know how to ask for the type of
service you need:

What is the postage rate for...?
Quel est le tarif de l'affranchissement pour...?
kehl eh luh tah-reef duh lah-frahN-shees-mahN poor

English	French	Pronunciation
a foreign country (for overseas)	l'étranger	*lay-trahN-zhay*
the United States	les États-Unis	*lay zay-tah zew-nee*
an air mail letter	une lettre envoyée par avion	*ewn lehtr ahN-vwah-yay pahr ah-vyohN*
a registered letter	une lettre recommandée	*ewn lehtr ruh-koh-mahN-day*
a special delivery letter	une lettre par exprès	*ewn lehtr pahr ehks-preh*

I would like to send this letter (this package).
Je voudrais envoyer cette lettre (ce paquet).
zhuh voo-dreh zahN-vwah-yay seht lehtr (suh pah-keh)

English	French	Pronunciation
by regular mail	par courrier régulier	*pahr koo-ryay ray-gew-lyay*
by air mail	par avion	*pahr ah-vyohN*
by special delivery	par exprès	*pahr ehks-preh*
C.O.D.	livrable contre remboursement (payable à l'arrivée)	*lee-vrahbl kohNtr rahN-boors-mahN (peh-yahbl ah lah-ree-vay)*

How much does this letter (package) weigh?
Combien pèse cette lettre (ce paquet)?
kohN-byaN pehz seht lehtr (suh pah-keh)

When will it arrive?
Quand arrivera-t-il (elle)?
kahN tah-ree-vrah teel (tehl)

Faxes, Photocopies, and Computers

If you want your business to run smoothly, you just can't do without these three essential items: faxes, photocopy machines, and computers. Use the phrases in the following sections to help you operate these machines in your business ventures.

Making Photocopies

I recently left the country to get some material for this book. I pestered a lot of people, but I got just about everything I needed. As luck would have it, when I went to the hotel's business center to have photocopies made, all the machines were down. Off I trudged to the nearest photocopy store. If this happens to you, here's what you might want to say:

I would like to make a photocopy of this paper
(this document).
Je voudrais faire une photocopie de ce papier
(ce document).
*zhuh voo-dreh fehr ewn foh-to-koh-pee duh suh pah-pyay
(suh doh-kew-mahN)*

What is the cost per page?
Quel est le prix par page?
kehl eh luh pree pahr pahzh

Can you enlarge it (by 50%)?
Pouvez-vous l'élargir (de cinquante pour cent)?
poo-vay voo lay-lahr-zheer (duh saN-kahNt poor sahN)

Can you reduce it (by 25%)
Pouvez-vous le réduire (de vingt-cinq pour cent)?
poo-vay vous luh ray-dweer (duh vaN-saNk poor sahN)

Can you make a color copy?
Pouvez-vous en faire une copie en couleurs?
poo-vay voo ahN fehr ewn koh-pee ahN koo-luhr

Fax It

Let's face it, a fax machine is becoming almost as important as a telephone in many households. Frankly, it still
boggles my mind that they are so easy to use. They can be
a real convenience, when you least expect it. When you
can transmit and receive messages and information in a
matter of seconds or minutes, you can speed up the time
it takes to transact business. That translates into extra
cash. If you are conducting business in a French-speaking
country, it's a must to be fax-literate.

Do you have a fax machine?
Avez-vous un télécopieur?
ah-vay voo uhN tay-lay-kohp-yuhr

I'd like to send a fax.
Je voudrais transmettre une télécopie.
zhuh voo-dreh trahNz-mehtr ewn tay-lay-koh-pee

May I fax this letter (document) (to you)?
Puis-je (vous) transmettre une télécopie de cette lettre
(de ce document)?
*pweezh (voo) trahNz-mehtr ewn koh-pee duh seht lehtr
(duh suh doh-kew-mahN)*

Fax it to me.
Envoyez-m'en (Envoie-m'en) une télécopie.
*ahN-vwah-yay mahN (ahN-vwah mahN) ewn
tay-lay-koh-pee*

I didn't get your fax.
Je n'ai pas reçu votre télécopie.
zhuh nay pah ruh-sew vohtr tay-lay-koh-pee

Did you receive my fax?
Avez-vous recçu ma télécopie?
ah-vay voo ruh-sew mah tay-lay-koh-pee

Your fax is illegible.
Votre télécopie n'est pas lisible.
vohtr tay-lay-koh-pee neh pah lee-zeebl

Please send it again.
Veuillez la transmettre de nouveau.
vuh-yay lah trahNz-mehtr duh noo-vo

Please confirm that you've received my fax.
Veuillez confirmer la réception de ma télécopie.
vuh-yay kohN-feer-may lah ray-sehp-syohN duh mah
tay-lay-koh-pee

I'm a Computer Geek

In today's fast-paced world you must have some computer
knowledge in order to conduct your business. It's important to know what system, programs, and peripherals
other businesses are using. Will your word processors and
spread sheets be compatible? Can you network? The
phrases that follow will help you, even if you're not a
computer geek.

What kind of computer do you have?
Quel système (type, genre) d'ordinateur avez-vous?
kehl sees-tehm (teep, zhahNr) dohr-dee-nah-tuhr ah-vay voo

What operating system are you using?
Quel système opérant employez-vous?
kehl sees-tehm oh-pay-rahN ahN-plwah-yay-voo

What word processing program are you using?
Quel système de traitement de texte employez-vous?
kehl sees-tehm duh treht-mahN duh tehkst
ahN-plwah-yay-voo

What spread sheet program are you using?
Quel tableur employez-vous?
kehl tah-bluhr ahN-plwah-yay-voo

What peripherals do you have?
Quels périphériques avez-vous?
kehl pay-ree-fay-reek ah-vay voo

Full Speed Ahead

For Internet access you would say: accéder à des données par consultation de serveurs en ligne.

To send e-mail you would say: faire un échange d'informations par messagerie électronique.

Chapter 15

Managing Your Money

In This Chapter

➤ Banking terms

➤ Banking expressions

This final chapter is for anyone who must make a trip to the bank—a tourist who has to change money, a business person with financial obligations, an investor in foreign affairs, or someone interested in purchasing a piece of property or a business.

At the Bank

There are many reasons for a person traveling or living abroad to go to a bank. The most common reason is to exchange money. (Banks do tend to give a very favorable rate of exchange.)

French banks can open anywhere between 8 a.m. and 9 p.m. and close between 3 p.m. and 5 p.m. Some banks close during the lunch break, which can last as long as two hours.

Money can also be changed at un **bureau de change**. These money exchanges can be found all over the streets of Paris and in other countries as well. Some offer excellent rates while others charge exorbitant commissions. It is always wise to check out a few before making a decision.

Attention!

Remember that the worst exchange rates are given by hotels, airports, and railway stations. Avoid them whenever possible.

Banking Transactions

If you have to go to the bank, the following phrases will be most helpful in common, everyday banking situations such as making deposits and withdrawals, opening a checking account, or taking out a loan.

What are the banking hours?
Quelles sont les heures d'ouverture et de fermeture?
kehl sohN lay zuhr doo-vehr-tewr ay duh fehr-muh-tewr

I would like…
Je voudrais…
zhuh voo-dreh

English	French	Pronunciation
to change some money	changer de l'argent	*shahN-zhay duh lahr-zhahN*
to cash a check	toucher un chèque	*too-shay uhN shehk*
to make a deposit	faire un dépôt (un versement)	*fehr un day-po (uhN vehrs-mahN)*
to make a payment	faire un paiement (un versement)	*fehr un peh-mahN (uhN vehrs-mahN)*
to make a withdrawal	faire un retrait	*fehr uhN ruh-treh*
to open an account	ouvrir un compte	*oo-vreer uhN kohNt*
to close an account	fermer un compte	*fehr-may uhN kohNt*
to take out a loan	faire un emprunt	*fehr uhN nahN-pruhN*

Will I get a monthly statement?
Est-ce que je recevrai un relevé mensuel?
ehs-kuh zhuh ruh-sehv-ray uhN ruh-lvay mahN-swehl

What is today's exchange rate?
Quel est le cours du change aujourd'hui?
kehl eh luh koor dew shahNzh o-zhoord-wee

Do you have an automatic teller machine?
Avez-vous un distributeur (guichet) automatique de billets?
ah-vay voo uhN dees-tree-bew-tuhr o-to-mah-teek duh bee-yeh

How does one use it?
Comment s'en sert-on?
kohN-mahN sahN sehr-tohN

Is it available all the time?
Est-il à ma disposition à tout moment sept jours sur sept?
eh-teel ah mah dees-po-zee-syohN ah too moh-mahN seht zhoor sewr seht

Can I take my money out 24 hours a day?
Puis-je faire des retraits d'argent vingt-quatre heures sur vingt-quatre?
pweezh fehr day ruh-treh dahr-zhahN vaN-kahtr uhr sewr vaN kahtr

Is there a commission fee for each transaction?
Y a-t-il une commission forfaitaire par opération?
ee ah-teel ewn koh-mee-syohN fohr-feh-tehr pahr oh-pay-rah-syohN

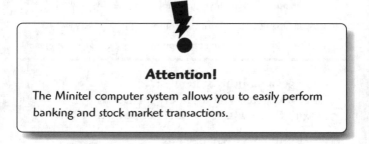

Attention!

The Minitel computer system allows you to easily perform banking and stock market transactions.

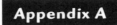
Verb Charts

Regular Verbs

-er Verbs
PARLER to speak
Past participle: parlé; Commands: Parle! Parlez!

Subj.	Present (is)	Imperfect (was)	Future (will)	Conditional (would)
je	parle	parlais	parlerai	parlerais
tu	parles	parlais	parleras	parlerais
il	parle	parlait	parlera	parlerait
nous	parlons	parlions	parlerons	parlerions
vous	parlez	parliez	parlerez	parleriez
ils	parlent	parlaient	parleront	parleraient

-ir Verbs
FINIR to finish
Past participle: fini; Commands: Finis! Finissez!

Subj.	Present (is)	Imperfect (was)	Future (will)	Conditional (would)
je	finis	finissais	finirai	finirais
tu	finis	finissais	finiras	finirais
il	finit	finissait	finira	finirait
nous	finissons	finissions	finirons	finirions
vous	finissez	finissiez	finirez	finiriez
ils	finissent	finissaient	finiront	finiraient

-re Verbs

VENDRE to sell
Past Participle: vendu; Commands: Vends! Vendez!

Subj.	Present (is)	Imperfect (was)	Future (will)	Conditional (would)
je	vends	vendais	vendrai	vendrais
tu	vends	vendais	vendras	vendrais
il	vend	vendait	vendra	vendrait
nous	vendons	vendions	vendrons	vendrions
vous	vendez	vendiez	vendrez	vendriez
ils	vendent	vendaient	vendront	vendraient

Irregular Verbs

*Verbs conjugated with être in the past tense are indicated by a *.

ALLER to go *
Past participle: allé; Commands: Va! Allez!

Subj.	Present	Subj.	Present
je	vais	nous	allons
tu	vas	vous	allez
il	va	ils	vont

AVOIR to have
Past participle: eu; Commands: Aie! Ayez!

Subj.	Present	Subj.	Present
je	ai	nous	avons
tu	as	vous	avez
il	a	ils	ont

BOIRE to drink
Past participle: bu; Commands: Bois! Buvez!

Subj.	Present	Subj.	Present
je	bois	nous	buvons
tu	bois	vous	buvez
il	boit	ils	boivent

CONNAÎTRE to know
Past participle: connu; Commands: Connais! Connaissez!

Subj.	Present	Subj.	Present
je	connais	nous	connaissons
tu	connais	vous	connaissez
il	connaît	ils	conaissent

DEVOIR to have to
Past participle: dû; Commands: Dois! Devez!

Subj.	Present	Subj.	Present
je	dois	nous	devons
tu	dois	vous	devez
il	doit	ils	doivent

DIRE to say, tell
Past participle: dit; Commands: Dis! Dites!

Subj.	Present	Subj.	Present
je	dis	nous	disons
tu	dis	vous	dites
il	dit	ils	disent

ÉCRIRE to write
Past participle: écrit; Commands: Écris! Écrivez!

Subj.	Present	Subj.	Present
je	écris	nous	écrivons
tu	écris	vous	écrivez
il	écrit	ils	écrivent

ÊTRE to be
Past participle: été; Commands: Sois! Soyez!

Subj.	Present	Subj.	Present
je	suis	nous	sommes
tu	es	vous	êtes
il	est	ils	sont

FAIRE to make, do
Past participle: fait; Commands: Fais! Faites!

Subj.	Present	Subj.	Present
je	fais	nous	faisons
tu	fais	vous	faites
il	fait	ils	font

LIRE to read
Past participle: lu; Commands: Lis! Lisez!

Subj.	Present	Subj.	Present
je	lis	nous	lisons
tu	lis	vous	lisez
il	lit	ils	lisent

METTRE to put
Past participle: mis; Commands: Mets! Mettez!

Subj.	Present	Subj.	Present
je	mets	nous	mettons
tu	mets	vous	mettez
il	met	ils	mettent

OUVRIR to open
Past participle: ouvert; Commands: Ouvre! Ouvrez!

Subj.	Present	Subj.	Present
je	ouvre	nous	ouvrons
tu	ouvres	vous	ouvrez
il	ouvre	ils	ouvrent

PARTIR to leave *
Past participle: parti; Commands: Pars! Partez!

Subj.	Present	Subj.	Present
je	pars	nous	partons
tu	pars	vous	partez
il	part	ils	partent

POUVOIR to be able to, can
Past participle: pu

Subj.	Present	Subj.	Present
je	peux	nous	pouvons
tu	peux	vous	pouvez
il	peut	ils	peuvent

PRENDRE to take
Past participle: pris; Commands: Prends! Prenez!

Subj.	Present	Subj.	Present
je	prends	nous	prenons
tu	prends	vous	prenez
il	prend	ils	prennent

RECEVOIR to receive
Past participle: reçu; Commands: Reçois! Recevez!

Subj.	Present	Subj.	Present
je	reçois	nous	recevons
tu	reçois	vous	recevez
il	reçoit	ils	reçoivent

SAVOIR to know
Past participle: su; Commands: Sache! Sachiez!

Subj.	Present	Subj.	Present
je	sais	nous	savons
tu	sais	vous	savez
il	sait	ils	savent

SORTIR to go out *
Past participle: sorti; Commands: Sors! Sortez!

Subj.	Present	Subj.	Present
je	sors	nous	sortons
tu	sors	vous	sortez
il	sort	ils	sortent

VENIR to come *
Past participle: venu; Commands: Viens! Venez!

Subj.	Present	Subj.	Present
je	viens	nous	venons
tu	viens	vous	venez
il	vient	ils	viennent

VOIR to see
Past participle: vu; Commands: Vois! Voyez!

Subj.	Present	Subj.	Present
je	vois	nous	voyons
tu	vois	vous	voyez
il	voit	ils	voient

VOULOIR to want
Past participle: voulu; Commands: Veuille! Veuillez!

Subj.	Present	Subj.	Present
je	veux	nous	voulons
tu	veux	vous	voulez
il	veut	ils	veulent

Appendix B

Useful Abbreviations and Emergency Phrases

Learning the following abbreviations will certainly help you get by:

Abbreviation	French	English
Cie.	compagnie	company
EU	États-Unis	United States
F	francs	francs
h.	heures	hour, o'clock
P et T	Postes et Télécommunications	Post Office and Telecommunication
RATP	Régie Autonome des Transports Parisiens	Parisian Transit Authority
SNCF	Société Nationale des Chemins de Fer	French National Railways
s.v.p.	s'il vous plaît	please

If you have any problems, these phrases will prove invaluable:

English	French	Pronunciation
Go away!	Allez-vous-en!	*ah-lay-voo-zahN*
Help!	Au secours!	*o suh-koor*
Help me!	Aidez-moi!	*eh-day mwah*
Hurry up!	Dépêchez-vous!	*day-peh-shay voo*
Look! Watch!	Regardez!	*ruh-gahr-day*
Listen!	Écoutez	*ay-koo-tay*
Wait!	Espérez!	*ehs-pay-ray*
Watch out!	Attention!	*ah-tahN-syohN*

Appendix C

English–French Dictionary

English	French	Pronunciation
A.M.	du matin	*dew mah-taN*
to able, be…to	pouvoir	*poo-vwahr*
about (the)	de (du, de la, de l')	*duh (dew, duh lah, de l)*
above	au-dessus de	*o duh-sew de*
across	à travers	*ah trah-vehr*
ad	annonce publicitaire (f.)	*ah-nohNs pew-blee-see-tehr*
afraid, be…(of)	avoir peur (de)	*ah-vwahr puhr (duh)*
after	après	*ah-preh*
afternoon (in the)	après-midi (m.) (de l')	*duh lah-preh mee-dee*
afterward	après, ensuite	*ah-preh, ahN-sweet*
again	encore	*ahN-kohr*
against	contre	*kohNtr*
ago (+ time)	il y a (+ time)	*eel yah*
to agree (with)	être d'accord (avec)	*ehtr dah-kohr (ah-vehk)*
air conditioning	climatisation (f.)	*klee-mah-tee-zah-syohN*
air letter	aérogramme (m.)	*ahy-roh-grahm*
airline	ligne aérienne (f.)	*lee-nyuh ahy-ryehn*
airplane	avion (m.)	*ah-vyohN*
airport	aéroport (m.)	*ahy-roh-pohr*
all	tout	*too*
almost	presque	*prehsk*
already	déjà	*day-zhah*
also	aussi	*o-see*

continues

English	French	Pronunciation
always	toujours	*too-zhoor*
to answer	répondre (à)	*ray-pohNdr ah*
any	de	*duh*
apple	pomme (f.)	*pohm*
April	avril (m.)	*ah-vreel*
area code	indicatif (m.)	*aN-dee-kah-teef*
to arrive	arriver	*ah-ree-vay*
ashtray	cendrier (m.)	*sahN-dree-yay*
to ask	demander	*duh-mahN-day*
aspirin	aspirine (f.)	*ah-spee-reen*
at	à	*ah*
August	août (m.)	*oo(t)*
autumn	automne (m.)	*o-tohn*
bad	mauvais	*mo-veh*
baggage claim area	bagages (m.)	*bah-gahzh*
bakery	boulangerie (f.)	*boo-lahNzh-ree*
ball-point pen	stylo à bille (m.)	*stee-lo ah beey*
band-aid	pansement adhésif (m.)	*pahNs-mahN ahd-ay-zeef*
bathing suit	maillot de bain (m.)	*mah-yod baN*
bathroom	toilettes (f. pl.), W.C. (m.)	*twah-leht, doobl-vay say*
to be	être	*ehtr*
beach	plage (f.)	*plahzh*
beautiful	beau (belle)	*bo (behl)*
bed	lit (m.)	*lee*
beef	boeuf (m.)	*buhf*
beer	bière (f.)	*byehr*
before	avant	*ah-vahN*

English	French	Pronunciation
to begin	commencer (à)	*koh-mahN-say*
behind	derrière, en arrière	*dehr-ryehr, ahN nah-ryehr*
to belong to	être à	*ehtr ah*
below	au-dessous de	*o duh-soo de*
belt	ceinture (f.)	*saN-tewr*
better	meilleur, mieux	*meh-yuhr, myuh*
between	entre	*ahNtr*
big	grand, gros(se)	*grahN, gro(s)*
black	noir(e)	*nwahr*
blanket	couverture (f.)	*koo-vehr-tewr*
blouse	chemisier (m.)	*shuh-meez-yay*
blue	bleu	*bluh*
boat	bateau (m.)	*bah-to*
book	livre (m.)	*leevr*
bookstore	librairie (f.)	*lee-breh-ree*
boot	botte (f.)	*boht*
booth (telephone)	cabine téléphonique (f.)	*kah-been tay-lay-foh-neek*
bowl	bol (m.)	*bohl*
box	boîte (f.)	*bwaht*
boy	garçon (m.)	*gahr-sohN*
bread	pain (m.)	*paN*
to bring (person)	amener	*ahm-nay*
to bring (thing)	apporter	*ah-pohr-tay*
to bring back	remporter	*rahN-pohr-tay*
brother	frère (m.)	*frehr*
brown	brun	*bruhN*
brush	brosse (f.)	*brohs*

continues

English	French	Pronunciation
bus stop	arrêt de bus (m.)	*ah-reh duh bews*
business center	centre d'affaires (m.)	*sahNtr dah-fehr*
butcher shop	boucherie (f.)	*boosh-ree*
butter	beurre (m.)	*buhr*
button	bouton (m.)	*boo-tohN*
by	par	*pahr*
cake	gâteau (m.)	*gah-to*
camera	appareil-photo (m.)	*ah-pah-rahy foh-to*
can	boîte (f.)	*bwaht*
candy	bonbon (m.)	*bohN-bohN*
candy store	confiserie (f.)	*kohN-feez-ree*
car	auto (f.), voiture (f.)	*o-to, vwah-tewr*
car rental	location de voitures (f.)	*loh-kah-syohN duh vwah-tewr*
card	carte (f.)	*kahrt*
carrot	carotte (f.)	*kah-roht*
carry	porter	*pohr-tay*
cart	chariot (m.)	*shah-ryoh*
to cash (check)	toucher	*too-shay*
cash register	caisse (f.)	*kehs*
castle	château (m.)	*shah-to*
chair	chaise (f.), siège (m.)	*shehz, syehzh*
cheese	fromage (m.)	*froh-mahzh*
chicken	poule (f.), poulet (m.)	*pool, poo-leh*
child	enfant (m. or f.)	*ahN-fahN*
to choose	choisir	*shwah-zeer*
church	église (f.)	*ay gleez*
to clean	propre	*prohpr*
to close	fermer	*fehr-may*

English	French	Pronunciation
clothing	vêtements (m.)	*veht-mahN*
coffee	café (m.)	*kah-fay*
cold	rhume (m.)	*rewm*
comb	peigne (m.)	*peh-nyuh*
contact lens	lentille (f.) de contact, verre (m.) de contact	*lahN-teey duh kohN-tahkt, vehr duh kohN-tahkt*
cookie	biscuit (m.)	*bees-kwee*
cooking	cuisine (f.)	*kwee-zeen*
corner	coin (m.)	*kwaN*
to cost	coûter	*koo-tay*
cough drops	pastilles (f.)	*pahs-teey*
cough syrup	sirop contre la toux (m.)	*see-roh kohNtr lah too*
counter	comptoir (m.)	*kohN-twahr*
cup	tasse (f.)	*tahss*
customs	douane (f.)	*doo-ahn*
dark	foncé	*fohN-say*
daughter	fille (f.)	*fee-y*
day	jour (m.)	*zhoor*
day after tomorrow	après-demain (m.)	*ah-preh duh-maN*
day before yesterday	avant-hier	*ah-vahN yehr*
December	décembre (m.)	*day-sahNbr*
delicatessen	charuterie (f.)	*shahr-kew-tree*
department store	grand magasin (m.)	*grahN mah-gah-zaN*
departure	départ (m.)	*day-pahr*
deposit box	coffre (m.)	*kohfr*
to dine	dîner	*dee-nay*
dirty	sale	*sahl*
to disturb	déranger	*day-rahN-zhay*

continues

English	French	Pronunciation
to do	faire	*fehr*
doctor	docteur (m.), médecin (m.)	*dohk-tuhr, mayd-saN*
dog	chien (m.)	*shyaN*
door	porte (f.)	*pohrt*
downtown	en ville	*ahN veel*
dozen	douzaine de	*doo-zehn duh*
dress	robe (f.)	*rohb*
to drink	boire	*bwahr*
drink	boisson (f.)	*bwah-sohN*
to dry clean	nettoyer à sec	*neh-twah-yay ah sehk*
dry cleaner's	teinturerie (f.)	*taN-tew-ruh-ree*
during	pendant	*pahN-dahN*
ear	oreille (f.)	*oh-rehy*
early	de bonne heure, tôt	*duh bohn uhr, to*
to earn	gagner	*gah-nyay*
earrings	boucles (f.) d'oreille	*bookl doh-rehy*
east	est (m.)	*ehst*
easy	facile	*fah-seel*
to eat	manger	*mahN-zhay*
egg	oeuf (m.)	*uhf*
eight	huit	*weet*
eighteen	dix-huit	*deez-weet*
eighty	quatre-vingts	*kahtr-vaN*
elevator	ascenseur (m.)	*ah-sahN-suhr*
eleven	onze	*ohNz*
embassy	ambassade (f.)	*ahN-bah-sahd*
to end	terminer	*tehr-mee-nay*
England	Angleterre (f.)	*ahN-gluh-tehr*

English	French	Pronunciation
enough	assez de	*ah-say duh*
to enter	entrer	*ahN-tray*
entrance	entrée (f.)	*ahN-tray*
every	tout	*too*
excuse me	pardon	*pahr-dohN*
exit	sortie (f.)	*sohr-tee*
expensive	cher (chère)	*shehr*
to explain	expliquer	*eks-plee-kay*
eye	oeil (m.) (pl. yeux)	*uhy (yuh)*
fall	automne (m.)	*o-tohn*
fantastic	génial	*zhay-nyahl*
far (from)	loin (de)	*lwaN (duh)*
father	père (m.)	*pehr*
favorite	favori(te)	*fah-voh-ree(t)*
fax	télécopie (f.)	*tay-lay-koh-pee*
February	février (m.)	*fay-vree-yay*
fifteen	quinze	*kaNz*
fifty	cinquante	*saN-kahNt*
find	trouver	*troo-vay*
to finish	achever, finir	*ah-shuh-vay, fee-neer*
fish store	poissonnerie (f.)	*pwah-sohn-ree*
five	cinq	*saNk*
floor (story)	étage (m.)	*ay-tahzh*
for	pour	*poor*
foreign	étranger (-ère)	*ay-trahN-zhay (yehr)*
to forget	oublier	*oo-blee-yay*
fork	fourchette (f.)	*foor-sheht*
forty	quarante	*kah-rahNt*

continues

English	French	Pronunciation
four	quatre	*kahtr*
fourteen	quatorze	*kah-tohrz*
French	français	*frahN-seh*
fresh	frais (fraîche)	*freh (frehsh)*
Friday	vendredi (m.)	*vahN-druh-dee*
friend	ami (m.)	*ah-mee*
from	de, de la, de l', des, du, en	*duh, duh lah, duh l, day, dew, ahN*
front, in...of	devant	*duh-vahN*
fruit store	fruiterie (f.)	*frwee-tree*
fun	amusant	*ah-mew-zahN*
funny	comique, drôle	*koh-meek, drohl*
game, to play a...of	faire une partie de	*fehr ewn pahr-tee duh*
gasoline	essence (f.)	*eh-sahNs*
gate	porte (f.)	*pohrt*
Germany	Allemagne (f.)	*ahl-mah-nyuh*
gift shop	boutique (f.)	*boo-teek*
girl	fille (f.)	*fee-y*
give	donner	*doh-nay*
to give back	rendre	*rahNdr*
glass	verre (m.)	*vehr*
glove	gant (m.)	*gahN*
to go	aller	*ah-lay*
good	bon(ne)	*bohN (bohn)*
good-bye	au revoir	*o ruh-vwahr*
gray	gris	*gree*
great	chouette, extra, formidable	*shoo-eht, ehks-trah, fohr-mee-dahbl*
green	vert	*vehr*

English	French	Pronunciation
grocery store	épicerie (f.)	*ay-pees-ree*
ground floor	rez-de-chaussée (m.)	*rayd-sho-say*
hair	cheveux (m.)	*shuh-vuh*
haircut	coupe de cheveux (f.)	*koop duh shuh-vuh*
ham	jambon (m.)	*zhahN-bohN*
hamburger	hamburger (m.)	*ahN-bewr-gehr*
hand	main (f.)	*maN*
hanger	cintre (m.)	*saNtr*
happy	heureux (-euse)	*uh-ruh(z)*
hat	chapeau (m.)	*shah-po*
to have	avoir	*ah-vwahr*
he	il	*eel*
to hear	entendre	*ahN-tahNdr*
hello	bonjour	*bohN-zhoor*
to help	aider	*eh-day*
her (to)	elle, la, sa, son, ses, (lui)	*ehl, lah, sah, sohN, say, (lwee)*
here	ici	*ee-see*
hi	salut	*sah-lew*
him, (to)	le (lui)	*luh, (lwee)*
his	sa, son, ses	*sah, sohN, say*
hour	heure (f.)	*uhr*
house	maison (f.)	*meh-zohN*
house, at the... (business) of	chez	*shay*
how	comment	*kohN-mahN*
how much, many	combien (de + noun)	*kohN-byaN (duh)*
hundred	cent	*sahN*
hungry, to be	avoir faim	*ah-vwahr faN*

continues

English	French	Pronunciation
husband	mari (m.)	*mah-ree*
I	je	*zhuh*
ice cream	glace (f.)	*glahs*
ice cubes	glaçons (m.)	*glah-sohN*
immediately	tout de suite	*toot sweet*
in	dans	*dahN*
information	renseignements (m.)	*rahN-seh-nyuh-mahN*
instead (of)	au lieu (de)	*o lyuh (duh)*
to invite	inviter	*aN-vee-tay*
it	le, la	*luh, lah*
it is	c'est	*seh*
January	janvier (m.)	*zhahN-vyay*
jar	bocal (m.)	*boh-kahl*
jewelry store	bijouterie (f.)	*bee-zhoo-tree*
juice	jus (m.), jus de + name of fruit	*zhew (duh)*
July	juillet (m.)	*zhwee-eh*
June	juin (m.)	*zhwaN*
to keep	garder	*gahr-day*
key	clé (clef) (f.)	*klay (klay)*
to know	savoir	*sah-vwahr*
to land (plane)	atterrir	*ah-teh-reer*
landing	palier (m.)	*pah-lyay*
last	dernier (-ère), passé(e)	*dehr-nyah (nyehr), pah-say*
late	tard	*tahr*
late (in arriving)	en retard	*ahN ruh-tahr*
laundry	blanchisserie (f.)	*blahN-shees-ree*
leather goods store	maroquinerie (f.)	*mah-roh-kaN-ree*

English	French	Pronunciation
to leave (behind)	partir, quitter, (laisser)	*pahr-teer, kee-tay, (leh-say)*
left, to the…(of)	à gauche (de)	*ah gosh (duh)*
lemon	citron (m.)	*see-trohN*
lend	prêter	*preh-tay*
less	moins	*mwaN*
letter	lettre (f.)	*lehtr*
lettuce	laitue (f.)	*leh-tew*
lighter	briquet (m.)	*bree-keh*
to like	aimer	*eh-may*
to listen (to)	écouter	*ay-koo-tay*
little	peu de	*puh duh*
to live (in)	demeurer, habiter	*duh-muh-ray, ah-bee-tay*
long	long(ue)	*lohN(g)*
to look at, watch	regarder	*ruh-guhr-day*
to look for	chercher	*shehr-shay*
to lose	perdre	*pehrdr*
lost and found	objets trouvés (m.)	*ohb-zheh troo-vay*
to love	aimer	*eh-may*
maid	fille de chambre (f.)	*fee-y duh shahNbr*
mailbox	boîte aux lettres (f.)	*bwaht o lehtr*
to make	faire	*fehr*
man	homme (m.)	*ohm*
manager	gérant (m.)	*zhay-rahN*
March	mars (m.)	*mahrs*
matter, it doesn't	n'importe	*nahN-pohrt*
May	mai (m.)	*meh*
me, (to)	moi, me	*mwah, muh*

continues

English	French	Pronunciation
mechanic	mécanicien(ne)	*may-kah-nee-syaN (syehn)*
medicine	médicament (m.)	*may-dee-kah-mahN*
to meet	faire la connaissance de, rencontrer, se réunir	*fehn lah koh-neh-sahNs duh, rahN-kohN-tray, suh ray-ew-neer*
menu	carte (f.), menu (m.)	*kahrt, muh-new*
merchandise	marchandise (f.)	*mahr-shahN-deez*
merchant	commerçant	*koh-mehr-sahN*
middle, in the…(of)	au milieu (de)	*o meel-yuh (duh)*
midnight	minuit (m.)	*nee-nwee*
milk	lait (m.)	*leh*
million	million (m.)	*meel-yohN*
mineral water carbonated non-carbonated	eau minérale (f.) gazeuse plate	*o mee-nay-rahl gah-zuhz plaht*
minute	minute (f.)	*mee-newt*
mirror	glace (f.), miroir (m.)	*glahs, meer-wahr*
Miss	mademoiselle (f.)	*mahd-mwah-zehl*
to miss	manquer, rater	*mahN-kay, rah-tay*
mistake	faute (f.), erreur (f.)	*foht, eh-ruhr*
Monday	lundi (m.)	*luhN-dee*
money	argent (m.)	*ahr-zhahN*
money exchange	bureau de change (m.)	*bew-ro duh shahNzh*
money order	mandat-poste (m.)	*mahN-dah pohst*
month	mois (m.)	*mwah*
more	plus	*plew*
morning, (in the)	matin (m.) (du)	*mah-taN (dew)*
mother	mère (f.)	*mehr*
Mr.	monsieur (m.)	*muh-syuh*

English	French	Pronunciation
Mrs.	madame (f.)	*mah-dahm*
much	beaucoup (de)	*bo-koo*
museum	musée (m.)	*mew-zay*
mushroom	champignon (m.)	*shahN-pee-nyohN*
mustard	moutarde (f.)	*moo-tahrd*
my	mes	*may*
napkin	serviette (f.)	*sehr-vyeht*
near	près (de)	*preh (duh)*
to need	avoir besoin (de)	*ah vwahr buh-zwaN (duh)*
never	ne...jamais	*nuh...zhah-meh*
new	neuf, nouveau (nouvelle)	*nuhf, noo-vo (noo-vehl)*
news	informations (f.)	*aN-fohr-mah-syohN*
newspaper	journal (m.)	*zhoor-nahl*
newsstand	kiosk à journaux (m.)	*kee-ohsk ah zhoor-noh*
next	prochain	*proh-shahN*
next to, beside	à côté (de)	*ah ko-tay (duh)*
nice	aimable, gentil(le), sympathique	*eh-mahbl, zhahN-tee-y, saN-pah-teek*
night	nuit (f.)	*nwee*
nightclub	boîte de nuit (f.), cabaret (m.)	*bwaht duh nwee, kah-bah-reh*
nine	neuf	*nuhf*
nineteen	dix-neuf	*deez-nuhf*
ninety	quatre-vingt-dix	*kahtr-vaN-dees*
no	non	*nohN*
no longer	ne...plus	*nuh...plew*
noon	midi (m.)	*mee-dee*
north	nord (m.)	*nohr*

continues

English	French	Pronunciation
nothing	ne...rien	*nuh...ryaN*
November	novembre (m.)	*noh-vahNbr*
now	maintenant	*maNt-nahN*
O.K.	d'accord, ça va	*dah-kohr, sah vah*
October	octobre (m.)	*ohk-tohbr*
of (the)	de, de la, de l', du, des	*duh, duh lah, duh l, dew*
of course	bien entendu, bien sûr	*byaN nahN-tahN-dew, byaN sewr*
often	souvent	*soo-vahN*
on	sur	*sewr*
one	on, un, une	*ohN, uhN, ewn*
only	seulement	*suhl-mahN*
open	ouvert	*oo-vehr*
opposite	en face (de)	*ahN fahs (duh)*
orange	orange (f.)	*oh-rahNzh*
to order	commander	*koh-mahN-day*
order, in...to	pour	*poor*
our	nos, notre	*no, nohtr*
out, to go	sortir	*sohr-teer*
P.M.	de l'après-midi	*duh lah-preh mee-dee*
package	paquet (m.)	*pah-keh*
pain	douleur (f.)	*doo-luhr*
pamphlet	brochure (f.)	*broh-shewr*
pants	pantalon (m.)	*luh pahN-tah-lohN*
paper	papier (m.)	*pah-pyay*
paper, toilet	papier hygiénique (m.)	*pahp-yay ee-zhyay-neek*
park	parc (m.)	*pahrk*
to pay, (for)	payer	*peh-yay*
pen (ball-point)	stylo à bille (m.)	*stee-lo ah beey*

English	French	Pronunciation
pencil	crayon (m.)	*kreh-yohN*
perfume store	parfumerie (f.)	*par-fewm-ree*
phone	téléphone (m.)	*tay-lay-fohn*
pillow	oreiller (m.)	*oh-reh-yay*
pills	pilules (f.)	*pee-lewl*
plate	assiette (f.)	*ah-syeht*
to play	jouer	*zhoo-ay*
please	s'il vous (te) plaît	*seel voo (tuh) pleh*
pocketbook	sac (à main) (m.)	*sahk (ah maN)*
police station	commissariat (m.) de police	*koh-mee-sah-ryah duh poh-lees*
pork	porc (m.)	*pohr*
porter	porteur (m.)	*pohr-tuhr*
post card	carte postale (f.)	*kahrt pohs-tahl*
postage	affranchissement(m.)	*ah-frahN-shees-mahN*
potato	pomme de terre (f.)	*pohm duh tehr*
pound of	demi-kilo de (m.), cinq cents grammes de	*duh-mee kee-lo duh, saNk sahN grahm duh*
prescription	ordonnance (f.)	*ohr-doh-nahNs*
pretty	joli	*zhoh-lee*
price	prix (m.), tarif (m.)	*pree, tah-reef*
problem	problème (m.)	*proh-blehm*
to put (on)	mettre	*mehtr*
quickly	vite	*veet*
rate	tarif (m.)	*tah-reef*
receipt	quittance (f.), reçu (m.)	*kee-tahNs, ruh-sew*
to receive	recevoir	*ruh-suh-vwahr*
red	rouge	*roozh*
to remain	rester	*rehs-tay*

continues

English	French	Pronunciation
to remove	enlever, ôter, quitter	*ahN-lvay, o-tay, kee-tay*
to repair	réparer	*ray-pah-ray*
to repeat	répéter	*ray-pay-tay*
to replace	remplacer	*rahN-plah-say*
to reserve	réserver	*ray-zehr-vay*
to return	rentrer, retourner	*rahN-tray, ruh-toor-nay*
to return (item)	rendre	*rahNdr*
rice	riz (m.)	*ree*
right, to be	avoir raison	*ah-vwahr reh-sohN*
right, to the (of)	à droite (de)	*ah drawht (duh)*
ring	bague (f.)	*bahg*
safe	coffre (m.)	*kohfr*
salesperson	vendeur (-euse)	*vahN-duhr (duhz)*
salt	sel (m.)	*sehl*
same, (all the)	mêhm, (tout de même)	*mehm, (too dmehm)*
Saturday	samedi (m.)	*sahm-dee*
to say	dire	*deer*
scissors	ciseaux (m.)	*see-zo*
seafood	fruits de mer (m.)	*frwee duh mehr*
seat	place (f.), siège (m.)	*plahs syehzh,*
second	deuxième, second(e)	*duhz-yehm, suh-gohN(d)*
to see	voir	*vwahr*
to sell	vendre	*vahNdr*
to send	envoyer	*ahN-vwah-yay*
September	septembre (m.)	*sehp-tahNbr*
to serve	servir	*sehr-veer*
seven	sept	*seht*
seventeen	dix-sept	*dee-seht*

English	French	Pronunciation
seventy	soixante-dix	*swah-sahNt-dees*
shampoo	shampooing (m.)	*shahN-pwaN*
she	elle	*ehl*
shirt (man-tailored)	chemise (f.)	*shuh-meez*
shoe repair person	cordonnier	*kohr-doh-nyay*
shoes	chaussures (f.), souliers (m.)	*sho-sewr, soo-lyay*
shopping, to go	faire des achats (emplettes)	*fehr day zah-shah (ahN-pleht)*
short	court	*koor*
show	spectacle (m.)	*spehk-tahkl*
shower	douche (f.)	*doosh*
shrimp	crevette (f.)	*kruh-veht*
sick	malade	*mah-lahd*
to sign	signer	*see-nyay*
silk	soie (f.)	*swah*
silver	argent (m.)	*ahr-zhahN*
since	depuis	*duh-pwee*
sister	soeur (f.)	*suhr*
six	six	*sees*
sixteen	seize	*sehz*
sixty	soixante	*swah-sahNt*
size	taille (f.)	*tahy*
skirt	jupe (f.)	*zhewp*
to sleep	dormir	*dohr-meer*
slice	tranche (f.)	*trahNsh*
slide	diapositive (f.)	*dee-ah-poh-zee-teev*
slowly	lentement	*lahNt-mahN*
small	petit	*puh-tee*

continues

English	French	Pronunciation
to smoke	fumer	*few-may*
sneakers	tennis (f.)	*tuh-nees*
soap, (bar of)	savon (m.), (savonnette) (f.)	*sah-vohN, (sah-voh-neht)*
socks	chaussettes (f.)	*sho-seht*
some	de, de la, de l', des, du	*duh, duh lah, duh l, day, dew*
sometimes	parfois, quelquefois	*pahr-fwah, kehl-kuh-fwah*
son	fils (m.)	*fees*
soon	bientôt, tôt	*byaN-to, to*
south	sud (m.)	*sewd*
souvenir shop	magasin de souvenirs (m.)	*mah-gah-zaN duh soo-vuh-neer*
Spain	Espagne (f.)	*ehs-pah-nyuh*
to speak	parler	*pahr-lay*
to spend (money)	dépenser	*day-pahN-say*
to spend (time)	passer	*pah-say*
spicy	épicé (f.)	*ay-pee-say*
spring	printemps (m.)	*praN-tahN*
stairs	escalier (m.)	*ehs-kah-lyay*
stamp	timbre (m.)	*taNbr*
stapler	agrafeuse (f.)	*ah-grah-fuhz*
stationery	papier à lettres (m.)	*pah-pyay ah lehtr*
to stay	rester	*rehs-tay*
steak	bifteck (m.)	*beef-tehk*
still	encore, toujours	*ahN-kohr, too-zhoor*
store	magasin (m.)	*mah-gah-zaN*
student	élève (m. or f.), étudiant (m.)	*ay-lehv, ay-tewd-yahN*

English	French	Pronunciation
subway	métro (m.)	*may-tro*
sugar	sucre (m.)	*sewkr*
suitcase	valise (f.)	*vah-leez*
summer	été (m.)	*ay-tay*
Sunday	dimanche (m.)	*dee-mahNsh*
sunglasses	lunettes de soleil (f.)	*lew-neht duh soh-lehy*
suntan oil	huile solaire (f.)	*weel soh-lehr*
supermarket	supermarché (m.)	*sew-pehr-mahr-shay*
sweet	doux (douce), sucré	*doo (doos), sew-kray*
to swim	nager	*nah-zhay*
Switzerland	Suisse (f.)	*swees*
table	table (f.)	*tahbl*
tailor	tailleur (m.)	*tah-yuhr*
to take	prendre	*prahNdr*
to take off	enlever	*ahN-lvay*
to take place	avoir lieu	*ah-vwahr lyuh*
takeoff (plane)	décollage (m.)	*day-koh-lahzh*
tea	thé (m.)	*tay*
teaspoon	cuiller (f.)	*kwee-yehr*
telephone book	annuaire (m.)	*ahn-wehr*
telephone number	numéro de téléphone (m.)	*new-may-ro duh tay-lay-fohn*
telephone, public	téléphone public (m.)	*tay-lay-fohn pew-bleek*
television	télévision (f.)	*tay-lay-vee-zyohN*
to tell	dire, raconter	*deer, rah-kohN-tay*
ten	dix	*dees*
that	ce, cet, cette. cela, que, ça	*suh, seht, seht, suh-lah, kuh, sah*
the	le, la, les	*luh, lah, lay*
their	leur(s)	*luhr*

continues

English	French	Pronunciation
them, (to)	les, elles, eux, (leur)	*lay, ehl, uh, (luhr)*
then	alors, ensuite, puis	*ah-lohrs, ahN-sweet, pwee*
there	là, y	*lah*
there is, are	il y a	*eel yah*
these	ces	*say*
they	ils, elles, on	*eel, ehl, ohN*
to think (about), (of)	penser (à), (de)	*pahN-say (ah), (duh)*
thirsty, be	avoir soif	*ah-vwahr swahf*
thirteen	treize	*trehz*
thirty	trente	*trahNt*
this	ce, cet, cette	*suh, seht, seht*
those	ces	*say*
thousand	mille (m.)	*meel*
three	trois	*trwah*
through	à travers, par	*ah trah-vehr, pahr*
Thursday	jeudi (m.)	*zhuh-dee*
ticket	billet (m.)	*bee-yeh*
time	temps (m.), heure (f.)	*tahN, uhr*
time, a long	longtemps	*lohN-tahN*
time, at the same	à la fois, en même temps	*ah lah fwah, ahN mehm than*
time, at what	à quelle heure	*ah kehl uhr*
time, to have the…to	avoir le temps de	*ah-vwahr luh tahN duh*
time, on	à l'heure, à temps	*ah luhr, ah tahN*
tissue	mouchoir en papier (m.)	*moosh-wahr ahN pah-pyay*
to	à	*ah*
to the	à la, à l', au, aux	*ah lah, ah l, o, o*

English	French	Pronunciation
today	aujourd'hui (m.)	*oh-zhoor-dwee*
together	ensemble	*ahN-sahNbl*
toilet paper	papier hygiénique (m.)	*pahp-yay ee-zhyay-neek*
token	jeton (m.)	*zheh-tohN*
tomorrow	demain (m.)	*duh-maN*
too	aussi	*o-see*
too much	trop (de)	*tro duh*
tooth	dent (f.)	*dahN*
toothache	rage (f.) de dents	*rahzh duh dahN*
toothbrush	brosse à dents (f.)	*brohs ah dahN*
toothpaste	pâte dentifrice (f.)	*paht dahN-tee-frees*
toward	vers	*vehr*
towel	serviette (f.)	*sehr-vyeht*
train	train (m.)	*traN*
transformer	transformateur (m.)	*trahs-fohr-mah-tuhr*
to travel	voyager	*vwah-yah-zhay*
trip, (to take a)	voyage (m.) (faire un)	*vwah-yahzh (fehr uhN)*
to try (to)	essayer (de)	*eh-say-yay (duh)*
Tuesday	mardi (m.)	*mahr-dee*
turkey	dinde (f.)	*daNd*
to turn	tourner	*toor-nay*
twelve	douze	*dooz*
twenty	vingt	*vaN*
two	deux	*duh*
umbrella	parapluie (m.)	*pah-rah-plwee*
under	sous	*soo*
to understand	comprendre	*kohN-prahNdr*
United States	États-Unis (m.)	*ay-tah zew-nee*

continues

English	French	Pronunciation
until	jusqu'à	*zhews-kah*
upstairs	en haut	*ahN o*
us, to us	nous	*noo*
value	valeur (f.)	*vah-luhr*
vanilla	vanille (f.)	*vah-neey*
VCR	magnétoscope (m.)	*mah-nyay-toh-skohp*
veal	veau (m.)	*vo*
vegetable	légume (m.)	*lay-gewm*
very	très	*treh*
to wait (for)	attendre	*ah-tahNdr*
wallet	portefeuille (m.)	*pohr-tuh-fuhy*
to want	vouloir	*voo-lwahr*
watch	montre (f.)	*mohNtr*
we	nous, on	*noo, ohN*
Wednesday	mercredi (m.)	*mehr-kruh-dee*
week	semaine (f.)	*suh-mehn*
to weigh	peser	*puh-zay*
well	bien	*byaN*
west	ouest (m.)	*wehst*
what	qu'est-ce que, que, quel(le), quoi	*kehs-kuh, kuh, kehl, kwah*
when	quand	*kahN*
where	où	*oo*
which	quel(le)(s)	*kehl*
which one	lequel, laquelle	*luh-kehl, lah-kehl*
white	blanc(he)	*blahN(sh)*
who, whom	qui	*kee*
why	pourquoi	*poor-kwah*

English	French	Pronunciation
wife	femme (f.)	*fahm*
window (ticket)	guichet (m.)	*gee-sheh*
wine	vin (m.)	*vaN*
winter	hiver (m.)	*ee-vehr*
to wish	souhaiter	*soo-eh-tay*
without	sans	*sahN*
woman	femme (f.)	*fahm*
wool	laine (f.)	*lehn*
to work	fonctionner, marcher, travailler	*fohNk-syoh-nay, mahr-shay, trah-vah-yay*
to wrap up	emballer	*ahN-bah-lay*
to write	écrire	*ay-kreer*
year	an (m.), année (f.)	*ahN, ah-nay*
years old, to be...	avoir...ans	*ah-vwahr...ahN*
yellow	jaune	*zhon*
yesterday	hier	*yehr*
yet	encore	*ahN-kohr*
you, (to)	on, toi, tu, te, vous	*ohN, twah, tew, tuh, voo*
your (fam.)	ta, ton, tes	*tah, tohN, tay*
your (pol.)	vos, votre	*vo, vohtr*
zoo	zoo (m.)	*zo*

French–English Dictionary

French	Pronunciation	English
à	*ah*	to, at
à tout à l'heure	*ah too tah luhr*	see you later
aider	*eh-day*	to help
ail (m.)	*ahy*	garlic
aimer	*eh-may*	to like, love
alcool (m.)	*ahl-kohl*	alcohol
aliments (m.)	*ah-lee-mahN*	food
Allemagne (f.)	*ahl-mah-nyuh*	Germany
aller	*ah-lay*	to go
alors	*ah-lohrs*	then
ami (m.)	*ah-mee*	friend
an (m.)	*ahN*	year
Angleterre (f.)	*ahN-gluh-tehr*	England
année (f.)	*ah-nay*	year
annuaire (m.)	*ahn-wehr*	telephone book
août (m.)	*oo(t)*	August
apporter	*ah-pohr-tay*	to bring
après	*ah-preh*	after, afterward
argent (m.)	*ahr-zhahN*	silver, money
arrêt de bus (m.)	*ah-reh duh bews*	bus stop
ascenseur (m.)	*ah-sahN-suhr*	elevator
assez de	*ah-say duh*	enough
assiette (f.)	*ah-syeht*	dinner plate
atelier (m.)	*ah-tuh-lyay*	studio
attendre	*ah-tahNdr*	to wait (for)
atterrir	*ah-teh-reer*	to land (plane)

French	Pronunciation	English
au	*o*	to the
au fond (de)	*o fohN (duh)*	at the bottom (back) (of)
au haut (de)	*o o (duh)*	in (at) the top (of)
au lieu (de)	*o lyuh (duh)*	instead (of)
au revoir	*o ruh-vwahr*	good-bye
au-dessous de	*o duh-soo de*	beneath, below
au-dessus de	*o duh-sew duh*	above, over
aujourd'hui (m.)	*oh-zhoor-dwee*	today
aussi	*o-see*	also, too
automne (m.)	*o-tohn*	autumn, fall
aux	*o*	to the
avant	*ah-vahN*	before
avertissement (m.)	*ah-vehr-tees-mahN*	warning
avion (m.)	*ah-vyohN*	airplane
avoir	*ah-vwahr*	to have
avoir besoin (de)	*ah-vwahr buh-zwaN duh*	need
avoir chaud	*ah-vwahr sho*	to be hot (person)
avoir envie (de)	*ah-vwahr ahN-vee (duh)*	to need
avoir faim	*ah-vwahr faN*	to be hungry
avoir froid	*ah-vwahr frwah*	to be cold (person)
avoir lieu	*ah-vwahr lyuh*	to take place
avoir mal à	*ah-vwahr mahl ah*	to have an ache in
avoir peur (de)	*ah-vwahr puhr (duh)*	to be afraid (of)
avoir raison	*ah-vwahr reh-sohN*	to be right
avoir soif	*ah-vwahr swahf*	to be thirsty
avoir sommeil	*ah-vwahr soh-mehy*	to be sleepy
avoir tort	*ah-vwahr tohr*	to be wrong

continues

French	Pronunciation	English
avoir...ans	*ah-vwahr...ahN*	to be...years old
avril (m.)	*ah-vreel*	April
bateau (m.)	*bah-to*	boat
beau (belle)	*bo (behl)*	handsome, beautiful
beaucoup (de)	*bo-koo (duh)*	much
beurre (m.)	*buhr*	butter
bien	*byaN*	well
bien sûr	*byaN sewr*	of course
bientôt	*byaN-to*	soon
bière (f.)	*byehr*	beer
bifteck (m.)	*beef-tehk*	steak
bijouterie (f.)	*bee-zhoo-tree*	jewelry store
billet (m.)	*bee-yeh*	ticket
blanc(he)	*blahN(sh)*	white
blanchisserie (f.)	*blahN-shees-ree*	laundry and dry cleaning service
bleu	*bluh*	blue, very rare
boeuf (m.)	*buhf*	beef
boire	*bwahr*	to drink
boisson (f.)	*bwah-sohN*	drink
boîte (f.)	*bwaht*	box, can
boîte aux lettres (f.)	*bwaht o lehtr*	mailbox
boîte de nuit (f.)	*bwaht duh nwee*	nightclub
bol (m.)	*bohl*	bowl
bon marché	*bohN mahr-shay*	cheap
bon(ne)	*bohN (bohn)*	good
bonbon (m.)	*bohN-bohN*	candy
bonjour	*bohN-zhoor*	Hello

French	Pronunciation	English
bonsoir	*bohN swahr*	Good evening
boucher (bouchère)	*boo-shay (boo-shehr)*	butcher
boulanger (-ère)	*boo-lahn-zhay (zhehr)*	baker
bouteille (f.)	*boo-tehy*	bottle
briquet (m.)	*bree-keh*	lighter
brosse (f.)	*brohs*	brush
brosse à dents (f.)	*brohs ah dahN*	toothbrush
brouillard (m.)	*broo-yahr*	fog
brun	*bruhN*	brown, brunette
bureau de change (m.)	*bew-ro duh shahNzh*	money exchange
bureau de tabac (m.)	*bew-ro duh tah-bah*	tobacconist
c'est	*seh*	it is
c'est entendu	*seh tahN-tahN-dew*	it's understood, agreed, all right
c'est-à-dire	*seh-tah-deer*	that is to say
ça	*sah*	that
ça va	*sah vah*	O.K.
caisse (f.)	*kehs*	cashier
canard (m.)	*kah-nard*	duck
carré d'agneau (m.)	*kah-ray dah-nyo*	rack of lamb
carte (f.)	*kahrt*	menu, card
carte postale (f.)	*kahrt pohs-tahl*	post card
ce	*suh*	this, that
ceinture (f.)	*saN-tewr*	belt
cela	*suh-lah*	that
cent	*sahN*	hundred
cerise (m.)	*suh-reez*	cherry
ces	*say*	these, those

continues

French	Pronunciation	English
cet	*seht*	this, that
cette	*seht*	this, that
chaise (f.)	*shehz*	chair
champignon (m.)	*shahN-pee-nyohN*	mushroom
chapeau (m.)	*shah-po*	hat
chariot (m.)	*shah-ryoh*	cart
charuterie (f.)	*shahr-kew-tree*	delicatessen
chaussettes (f.)	*sho-seht*	socks
chaussures (f.)	*sho-sewr*	shoes
chemise (f.)	*shuh-meez*	shirt (man-tailored)
chemisier (m.)	*shuh-meez-yay*	blouse
cher (chère)	*shehr*	dear, expensive
chercher	*shehr-shay*	to look for
cheveux (m.)	*shuh-vuh*	hair
chez	*shay*	at the house (business) of
choisir	*shwah-zeer*	to choose
chouette	*shoo-eht*	great
cinq	*saNk*	five
cinquante	*saN-kahNt*	fifty
cintre (m.)	*saNtr*	hanger
ciseaux (m.)	*see-zo*	scissors
citron (m.)	*see-trohN*	lemon
citron pressé (m.)	*see-trohN preh-say*	lemonade
clé (clef)	*klay (klay)*	key
coffre (m.)	*kohfr*	trunk, safe (deposit box)
coiffeur (coiffeuse)	*kwah-fuhr (kwah-fuhz)*	hairdresser
combien (de + noun)	*kohN-byaN (duh)*	how much, many

French	Pronunciation	English
comme	*kohm*	as
commencer (à)	*koh-mahN-say (ah)*	to begin
comment	*kohN-mahN*	how
comprendre	*kohN-prahNdr*	to understand
confiserie (f.)	*kohN-feez-ree*	candy store
confiture (f.)	*kohN-fee-tewr*	jam, jelly
connaître	*koh-nehtr*	to be acquainted with
court	*koor*	short
couteau (m.)	*koo-to*	knife
coûter	*koo-tay*	to cost
couverture (f.)	*koo-vehr-tewr*	blanket
cravate (f.)	*krah-vaht*	tie
crayon (m.)	*kreh-yohN*	pencil
crevette (f.)	*kruh-veht*	shrimp
cuir (m.)	*kweer*	leather
d'accord	*dah-kohr*	agreed, O.K.
d'ailleurs	*dah-yuhr*	besides, moreover
dans	*dahN*	in
de	*duh*	from, of, about, any
de bonne heure	*duh bohn uhr*	early
décollage (m.)	*day-koh-luhzh*	takeoff
défendre	*day-fahNdr*	to defend, prohibit
déjà	*day-zhah*	already
déjeuner (m.)	*day-zhuh-nay*	to eat lunch
demain (m.)	*duh-maN*	tomorrow
dentifrice (m.)	*dahN-tee-frees*	mouthwash
dépenser	*day-pahN-say*	spend (money)

continues

French	Pronunciation	English
depuis	*duh-pwee*	since
dernier (-ère)	*dehr-nyah (nyehr)*	last
derrière	*dehr-ryehr*	behind
des	*day*	from, of, about (the), some
deux	*duh*	two
devant	*duh-vahN*	in front of
devoir	*duh-vwahr*	to have to
dimanche (m.)	*dee-mahNsh*	Sunday
dinde (f.)	*daNd*	turkey
dire	*deer*	to say, tell
dix	*dees*	ten
dix-huit	*deez-weet*	eighteen
dix-neuf	*deez-nuhf*	nineteen
dix-sept	*dee-seht*	seventeen
donner	*doh-nay*	to give
donner sur	*doh-nay sewr*	to face
dormir	*dohr-meer*	to sleep
douane (f.)	*doo-ahn*	customs
douche (f.)	*doosh*	shower
douze	*dooz*	twelve
du	*dew*	from, of, about (the), some
écouter	*ay-koo-tay*	to listen (to)
écrire	*ay-kreer*	to write
église (f.)	*ay gleez*	church
elle	*ehl*	she, her
elles	*ehl*	they, them
en	*ahN*	some, about, from, of it, them

French	Pronunciation	English
encore	*ahN-kohr*	still, yet, again
enfant (m. or f.)	*ahN-fahN*	child
enfin	*ahN-faN*	finally, at last
enlever	*ahN-lvay*	to take off, remove
ensemble	*ahN-sahNbl*	together
ensuite	*ahN-sweet*	then, afterwards
entendre	*ahN-tahNdr*	to hear
entier (-ère)	*ahN-tyay (yehr)*	entire
entre	*ahNtr*	between
envoyer	*ahN-vwah-yay*	to send
épicier (-ère)	*ay-pee-syay (yehr)*	grocer
escale (f.)	*ehs-kahl*	stopover
escalier (m.)	*ehs-kah-lyay*	stairs
Espagne (f.)	*ehs-pah-nyuh*	Spain
espérer	*ehs-pay-ray*	to hope
essayer (de)	*eh-say-yay (duh)*	to try (to)
essence (f.)	*eh-sahNs*	gasoline
est (m.)	*ehst*	east
étage (m.)	*ay-tahzh*	floor (story)
États-Unis (m.)	*ay-tah zew-nee*	United States
été (m.)	*ay-tay*	summer
étiquette (f.)	*ay-tee-keht*	identification tag
étranger (-ère)	*ay-trahN-zhay (yehr)*	foreign
être	*ehtr*	to be
être à	*ehtr ah*	to belong to
être d'accord (avec)	*ehtr dah-kohr*	to agree (with)
eux	*uh*	them
facile	*fah-seel*	easy

continues

French	Pronunciation	English
faire	*fehr*	to make, do
faux (fausse)	*fo (fos)*	false
femme (f.)	*fahm*	woman, wife
fenêtre (f.)	*fuh-nehtr*	window
fermer	*fehr-may*	to close
fêter	*feh-tay*	to celebrate
février (m.)	*fay-vree-yay*	February
fille (f.)	*fee-y*	daughter, girl
fils (m.)	*fees*	son
finir	*fee-neer*	to finish
fourchette (f.)	*foor-sheht*	fork
frais (fraîche)	*freh (frehsh)*	fresh
fraise (f.)	*frehz*	strawberry
framboise (f.)	*frahN-bwahz*	raspberry
français	*frahN-seh*	French
frère (m.)	*frehr*	brother
fromage (m.)	*froh-mahzh*	cheese
fruits de mer (m.)	*frwee duh mehr*	seafood
fumer	*few-may*	to smoke
gagner	*gah-nyay*	to win, earn
garçon (m.)	*gahr-sohN*	boy, waiter
gâteau (m.)	*gah-to*	cake
gazeux (-euse)	*gah-zuh(z)*	carbonated
gérant (m.)	*zhay-rahN*	manager
glace (f.)	*glahs*	ice cream, mirror
glaçons (m.)	*glah-sohN*	ice cubes
grand	*grahN*	big
gris	*gree*	gray

French	Pronunciation	English
guichet (m.)	*gee-sheh*	window
heure (f.)	*uhr*	hour
hier	*yehr*	yesterday
hiver (m.)	*ee-vehr*	winter
homard (m.)	*oh-mahr*	lobster
homme (m.)	*ohm*	man
huit	*weet*	eight
huître (f.)	*weetr*	oyster
hypermarché (m.)	*ee-pehr-mahr-shay*	large supermarket
ici	*ee-see*	here
il	*eel*	he
il y a (+ time)	*eel yah*	there is, are; ago (+ time)
ils	*eel*	they
immeuble (m.)	*ee-muhbl*	apartment building
imperméable (m.)	*aN-pehr-may-ahbl*	raincoat
jamais	*zhah-meh*	never, ever
jambon (m.)	*zhahN-bohN*	ham
janvier (m.)	*zhahN-vyay*	January
jaune	*zhon*	yellow
je	*zhuh*	I
jeudi (m.)	*zhuh-dee*	Thursday
joli	*zhoh-lee*	pretty
jouer	*zhoo-ay*	to play, gamble
jour (m.)	*zhoor*	day
journal (m.)	*zhoor-nahl*	newspaper
juillet (m.)	*zhwee-eh*	July
juin (m.)	*zhwaN*	June

continues

French	Pronunciation	English
jupe (f.)	*zhewp*	skirt
jus de (+ name of fruit)	*zhew duh*	fruit juice (m.)
kiosk à journaux (m.)	*kee-ohsk ah zhoor-noh*	newsstand
la	*lah*	the, her, it
là	*lah*	there
laisser	*leh-say*	to leave (behind)
lait (m.)	*leh*	milk
laitue (f.)	*leh-tew*	lettuce
laquelle	*lah-kehl*	which one
le	*luh*	the, him, it
légume (m.)	*lay-gewm*	vegetable
lentement	*lahNt-mahN*	slowly
lequelle	*luh-kehl*	which one
les	*lay*	the, them
lettre (f.)	*lehtr*	letter
leurs	*luhr*	their
librairie (f.)	*lee-breh-ree*	bookstore
lire	*leer*	to read
lit (m.)	*lee*	bed
livre (m.)	*leevr*	book
location de voitures (f.)	*loh-kah-syohN duh vwah-tewr*	car rental
loin (de)	*lwaN (duh)*	far (from)
longtemps	*lohN-tahN*	a long time
louer	*loo-ay*	to rent
lourd	*loor*	heavy
lui	*lwee*	him, to him, her
lundi (m.)	*luhN-dee*	Monday

French	Pronunciation	English
lunettes de soleil (f.)	*lew-neht duh soh-lehy*	sunglasses
madame (f.)	*mah-dahm*	Mrs.
mademoiselle (f.)	*mahd-mwah-zehl*	Miss
magasin (m.)	*mah-gah-zaN*	store
mai (m.)	*meh*	May
maillot de bain (m.)	*mah-yod baN*	bathing suit
main (f.)	*maN*	hand
maintenant	*maNt-nahN*	now
maison (f.)	*meh zohN*	house
malade	*mah-lahd*	sick
manger	*mahN-zhay*	to eat
manteau (m.)	*mahN-to*	overcoat
maquillage (m.)	*mah-kee-yahzh*	makeup
mardi (m.)	*mahr-dee*	Tuesday
mari (m.)	*mah-ree*	husband
maroquinerie (f.)	*mah-roh-kuN-ree*	leather goods store
mars (m.)	*mahrs*	March
mauvais	*mo-veh*	bad
me	*muh*	me, to me
médecin (m.)	*mayd-saN*	doctor
médicament (m.)	*may-dee-kah-mahN*	medicine
meilleur	*mch-yuhr*	better
même	*mehm*	even
mer (f.)	*mehr*	sea
mercredi (m.)	*mehr-kruh-dee*	Wednesday
mère (f.)	*mehr*	mother
mes	*may*	my
météo (f.)	*may-tay-o*	weather

continues

French	Pronunciation	English
métro (m.)	*may-tro*	subway
mettre	*mehtr*	put (on)
midi (m.)	*mee-dee*	noon
mieux	*myuh*	better
mille (m.)	*meel*	thousand
minuit (m.)	*mee-nwee*	midnight
moi	*mwah*	me, I
moins	*mwaN*	less
mois	*mwah*	month
monsieur (m.)	*muh-syuh*	Mr.
monter	*mohN-tay*	to go up
montre (f.)	*mohNtr*	watch
montrer	*mohN-tray*	to show
musée (m.)	*mew-zay*	museum
n'est-ce pas	*nehs-pah*	isn't that so
n'importe	*nahN-pohrt*	it doesn't matter
ne…jamais	*nuh…zhah-meh*	never
ne…plus	*nuh…plew*	no longer
ne…rien	*nuh…ryaN*	nothing, anything
neige (f.)	*nehzh*	snow
nettoyer	*neh-twah-yay*	to clean
neuf	*nuhf*	nine
noir(e)	*nwahr*	black
noix (f.)	*nwah*	walnut
nord (m.)	*nohr*	north
nos	*no*	our
notre	*nohtr*	our
nous	*noo*	we, us, to us

French	Pronunciation	English
nouveau (nouvelle)	*noo-vo (noo-vehl)*	new
novembre (m.)	*noh-vahNbr*	November
nuage (m.)	*new-ahzh*	cloud
objets trouvés (m.)	*ohb-zheh troo-vay*	lost and found
octobre (m.)	*ohk-tohbr*	October
oeuf (m.)	*uhf*	eggs
oignon (m.)	*oh-nyohN*	onion
on	*ohN*	one, we, they, you
onze	*ohNz*	eleven
or (m.)	*ohr*	gold
orage (m.)	*oh-rahzh*	storms
où	*oo*	where
ouest (m.)	*wehst*	west
ouvert	*oo-vehr*	open
pain (m.)	*paN*	bread
pantalon (m.)	*pahN tah-lohN*	pants
par	*pahr*	by, through, per
parapluie (m.)	*puh-rah-plwee*	umbrella
parfois	*pahr-fwah*	sometimes
parler	*pahr-lay*	to speak
partir	*pahr-teer*	to leave
pendant	*pahN-duhN*	during
penser (à) (de)	*pahN-say ah*	to think (about) (of)
perdre	*pehrdr*	lose
père (m.)	*pehr*	father
petit	*puh-tee*	small
peu (de)	*puh duh*	little
piscine (f.)	*pee-seen*	swimming pool

continues

French	Pronunciation	English
plage (f.)	*plahzh*	beach
pluie	*plwee*	rain
plus	*plew*	more
pneu (m.)	*pnuh*	tire
poisson (m.)	*pwah-sohN*	fish
poivre (m.)	*pwahvr*	pepper
pomme (f.)	*pohm*	apple
pomme de terre (f.)	*pohm duh tehr*	potato
porte (f.)	*pohrt*	door, gate
portefeuille (m.)	*pohr-tuh-fuhy*	wallet
porter	*pohr-tay*	wear, carry
porteur (m.)	*pohr-tuhr*	porter
portier (m.)	*pohr-tyay*	doorman
poulet (m.)	*poo-leh*	chicken
pour	*poor*	for, in order to
pourquoi	*poor-kwah*	why
pouvoir	*poo-vwahr*	to be able to
premier (-ère)	*pruh-myay (yehr)*	first
prendre	*prahNdr*	to take
près (de)	*preh (duh)*	near
presque	*prehsk*	almost
prêter	*preh-tay*	to lend
printemps (m.)	*praN-tahN*	spring
prix (m.)	*pree*	price
prochain	*proh-shahN*	next
propre	*prohpr*	clean
puis	*pwee*	then
qu'est-ce que	*kehs-kuh*	what

French	Pronunciation	English
quand	*kahN*	when
quarante	*kah-rahNt*	forty
quatorze	*kah-tohrz*	fourteen
quatre	*kahtr*	four
quatre-vingt-dix	*kahtr-vaN-dees*	ninety
quatre-vingts	*kahtr-vaN*	eighty
que	*kuh*	that, what
quel(le)(s)	*kehl*	which, what
quelquefois	*kehl-kuh-fwah*	sometimes
qui	*kee*	who, whom
quinze	*kaNz*	fifteen
recevoir	*ruh-suh-vwahr*	to receive
reçu (m.)	*ruh-sew*	receipt
regarder	*ruh-gahr-day*	to look at, watch
rencontrer	*ruhN-kohN-tray*	to meet
rendre	*rahNdr*	to give back, return
renseignements (m.)	*rahN-seh-nyuh-mahN*	information
rentrer	*rahN-tray*	to return
réparer	*ray-pah-ray*	to repair
répéter	*ray-pay-tay*	to repeat
répondre (à)	*ray-pohNdr ah*	to answer
rester	*rehs-tay*	to stay, remain
rez-de-chaussée (m.)	*rayd-sho-say*	ground floor
robe (f.)	*rohb*	dress
rouge	*roozh*	red
sa	*sah*	his, her
sac (à main) (m.)	*sahk (ah maN)*	pocketbook
salle (f.)	*sahl*	room

continues

French	Pronunciation	English
saluer	*sah-lew-ay*	greet
salut	*sah-lew*	Hi
samedi (m.)	*sahm-dee*	Saturday
sans	*sahN*	without
sans doute	*sahN doot*	without a doubt
savoir	*sah-vwahr*	to know
savon (m.)	*sah-vohN*	soap
savonnette (f.)	*sah-voh-neht*	bar of soap
se	*suh*	to him (her) (them) self (selves)
seize	*sehz*	sixteen
sel (m.)	*sehl*	salt
semaine (f.)	*suh-mehn*	week
sembler	*sahN-blay*	seem
sept	*seht*	seven
septembre (m.)	*sehp-tahNbr*	September
ses	*say*	his, her
seulement	*suhl-mahN*	only
siège (m.)	*syehzh*	chair, seat
six	*sees*	six
soeur (f.)	*suhr*	sister
soi	*swah*	oneself
soixante	*swah-sahNt*	sixty
soixante-dix	*swah-sahNt-dees*	seventy
soleil (m.)	*soh-lehy*	sun
son	*sohN*	his, her
sortie (f.)	*sohr-tee*	exit
sortie de secours (f.)	*sohr-tee duh suh-koor*	emergency exit

French	Pronunciation	English
sortir	*sohr-teer*	to go out
souhaiter	*soo-eh-tay*	to wish
souliers (m.)	*soo-lyay*	shoes
sous	*soo*	under
sous-sol (m.)	*soo-sohl*	basement
souvent	*soo-vahN*	often
sucre (m.)	*sewkr*	sugar
sud (m.)	*sewd*	south
sur	*sewr*	on
sympathique	*saN-pah-teek*	nice
ta	*tah*	your (fam.)
tailleur (m.)	*tah-yuhr*	tailor, suit
tard	*tahr*	late
tarif (m.)	*tah-reef*	price, rate
te	*tuh*	you, to you
tempête (f.)	*tahN-peht*	storm
terre (f.)	*tehr*	land
tes	*tay*	your (fam.)
timbre (m.)	*taNbr*	stamp
tirer	*tee-ray*	to pull, shoot
toi	*twah*	you
ton	*tohN*	your (fam.)
tôt	*to*	soon, early
toujours	*too-zhoor*	always, still
tout	*too*	quite, entirely, all, every
tout à coup	*too tah koo*	suddenly
tout à fait	*too tah feh*	entirely

continues

French	Pronunciation	English
tout de suite	*toot sweet*	immediately
tout droit	*too drwah*	straight ahead
tout près	*too preh*	nearby
tranche (f.)	*trahNsh*	slice
travailler	*trah-vah-yay*	to work
traverser	*trah-vehr-say*	to cross
treize	*trehz*	thirteen
trente	*trahNt*	thirty
très	*treh*	very
trois	*trwah*	three
trop (de)	*tro (duh)*	too much
trouver	*troo-vay*	to find
tu	*tew*	you
un, une	*uhN, ewn*	one
valoir la peine (de)	*vah-lwahr lah pehn (duh)*	to be worthwhile
valoir mieux	*vahl-vwahr myuh*	to be better
veau (m.)	*vo*	veal
veille (f.)	*vehy*	eve
vendredi (m.)	*vahN-druh-dee*	Friday
vent (m.)	*vaN*	wind
verre (m.)	*vehr*	lens, glass
vers	*vehr*	toward
vert	*vehr*	green
vêtements (m.)	*veht-mahN*	clothing
viande (f.)	*vyahNd*	meat
vide	*veed*	empty
vieux (vieille)	*vyuh (vyay)*	old
vin (m.)	*vaN*	wine

French	Pronunciation	English
vingt	*vaN*	twenty
vite	*veet*	quickly
voir	*vwahr*	to see
voiture (f.)	*vwah-tewr*	car
vol (m.)	*vohl*	flight
volaille (f.)	*voh-lahy*	poultry
vos	*vo*	your (pol.)
votre	*vohtr*	your (pol.)
vouloir	*voo-lwahr*	to want
vous	*voo*	you, to you
vraiment	*vreh-mahN*	really, truly
W.C. (m.)	*doobl-vay say*	bathroom, toilet facilities
y	*ee*	there

Index

J-L

M